Written in the Rainbow:
A Woman's Secret to Self-Esteem

by
Almira Ross & Susie Heath

WRITTEN IN THE RAINBOW

© 2008 Almira Ross and Susie Heath. All rights reserved.

First published 06/30/2008

Ecademy Press
6 Woodland Rise, Penryn,
Cornwall UK TR10 8QD
info@ecademy-press.com
www.ecademy-press.com

ISBN: 978-1-905823-35-2 (sc)

Printed and Bound by;
Lightning Source in the UK and USA

This book is printed on acid-free paper from managed forests. This book is printed on demand, so no copies will remaindered or pulped.

Table of Contents

Preface

The book you now hold in your hand is a treasure trove to help you on your way to creating your life the way you really want, without fear, without judgement, without any part of you holding you back.

A Woman's Secret to Self-Esteem is the first in a series of **Written in the Rainbow** books dedicated to women who work.

Why "Secret?" Because as women, so many of us secretly suffer from low self-esteem in several areas of our lives, and we cover it up by trying harder, and by putting on a false mask to hide behind. We fail to realise our full potential because we're afraid of being found out, of not being good enough, clever enough, qualified enough, attractive enough, worthy enough. The list is endless. But we're here to give you the secrets to unlock your amazing potential.

Why Rainbow? Because this book takes us from the real fears, phobias and anxieties which hold us back, (what we call the red stuff) through the journey of learning and growth and understanding, to the other end of the rainbow, the place where we feel more peaceful and centred. We travel through the whole spectrum of colours.

Why Women's Secret? Because as women, we want to bring to you information that speaks to your heart, to really make a difference, using language which women relate to – recognizing and acknowledging that the structure of our bodies and even our brains is very different from men.

As women, we have certain natural gifts that are hard-wired into our brain chemistry: for example, our ability to connect deeply with others at a far more intuitive and sensitive level than men, the easy way we can read emotion in faces and tones of voice, our ability to defuse conflict. These are all part of our inheritance, and we have unique and different skills and abilities. It's who we are.

Working with women in our coaching practices for more than ten years, we've discovered a few simple truths. Beneath the desire to look good, to be loved, cherished and respected is an underlying belief system that eats away at us, because we women take things so much to heart. It's all about the way we think – nothing more, nothing less – and our belief system becomes the truth by which we live each day of our lives.

It's a truth that often says *"I am unworthy"*; *"I don't deserve any better"*; *"I'm always wrong"*; *"I haven't got what it takes, so why bother?"*

Our culture teaches us that we need to do more, have more, be more; and we can't help but compare ourselves to the glamorous celebrities who adorn our magazines and television screens. It teaches us that whatever we do, we're still not quite good enough, and this has far reaching effects on our self-esteem, constantly niggling away at us from all directions. We compare ourselves to that perfect woman over our shoulder, and fail to match up – and fail to reward ourselves for what we have already achieved.

And it's been the story of our lives too, for longer than we'd like to admit. Like many women in the 20th century, we learned at a very early age to put everybody else first – father, brother, husband, boss, children – and make do with the leftovers for ourselves, because that was what we were taught by our female role-models: our mothers, our aunts, our grannies, our teachers. We took on board a learning that said we were useless, or stupid, that we'd never amount to much, or go very far. We learned to fear being caught out, to fear the humiliation of being exposed, of not being good enough, pretty enough or clever enough, and to feel a consequent fear of rejection.

As women we learn to find fault with our bodies, to be ashamed of the natural rhythms that course through us each month, to resent the ups and downs of our menstrual cycles. And when confronted by irritability and uncontrollable mood swings brought on by the drop in hormone levels, we think it's our fault – we feel we ought to be able to control our emotions. We want to hide these female problems from our colleagues at work who see us as weak.

At work, it has been discovered that when women look at the requirements for a new job and realise they can do about 60% of them, they decide not to apply because they feel they're not qualified or experienced enough. Interestingly though, a man in the same position would apply for – and probably get – the job. Often we sell ourselves short because we don't value ourselves enough.

We learn so much that doesn't serve us, and then we work extra hard to compensate for these feelings of inadequacy and to prove ourselves worthy, to prove that women are no fading wall-flowers, but strong, powerful, capable leaders, even if this means enduring difficult situations, compromising our health, or even staying in abusive relationships.

When we are born, our self-esteem is intact. All the unhelpful learning happens between birth and about six years old. Like it or not, it's hard-wired into our minds, where it will continue to govern our lives until the day we die – unless we decide to un-learn it and re-wire our minds. This is possible. Indeed, it can be an easy and effortless process. Once you understand how your mind works and what you can do to take control of your mind, you'll make profound and lasting changes to your thinking and your life.

Individually and collectively, we have both been on a long but immensely rewarding journey of learning, of self-development and self-discovery, and thankfully, both of us have found our own way of recovering our self-esteem and living rich and fulfilling lives. It has given us insights and amazing tools, together with a life-long commitment to help others like you rediscover and restore your self-esteem.

This book is full of activities, exercises and games that have helped us greatly in rebuilding our own self-esteem. We've learned them over many years of experimenting, and have selected the most powerful and effective ones to include here. We know they are the key that will create powerful changes for you. When you can take the time to complete these exercises and activities, you will uncover, rediscover and learn to value your precious sense of self, and celebrate the new life your improved self-esteem brings to you.

Introduction

Introduction

What is self-esteem? And what can women do to change, to recover their sense of self and live satisfying and fulfilled lives?

To esteem another is to respect her and hold her in high regard. Thus, self-esteem is the practice of respecting yourself; it's holding yourself – all that you are, all that you have been, and all that you may ever become – in high regard. It's knowing deep inside that you are a woman of value; it's knowing that you matter, that who you are and what you do make a difference in the world. And for so many of us, this means giving ourselves permission to love and nurture ourselves, so that we can come to know, to acknowledge, and to express our personal, feminine power and allow ourselves to become the women we were born to be.

Everything we do in our lives is a reflection of our self-esteem: the quality of our health, our relationships, our wealth, our day-to-day life and our creativity. That is why this book is so important and why nurturing and developing a healthy sense of self and of self-respect is so essential to your well-being. Everything we do is a choice – not to do anything is also a choice. So you have a choice right here, right now.

Many courses in training and personal development in business today are created and presented by men; these are often not appropriate for women as they are too insensitive for the inner core of who we really are, and they leave us wanting – feeling even more inadequate as we fail to keep up with their masculine force. Consequently we strive to become more masculine in our habits and behaviour, even when it comes to developing our inner selves. That's why it's so important that this work is created <u>by</u> women <u>for</u> women, recovering our powerful and innately intuitive feminine essence.

There is a huge untapped well of feminine potential that is not being addressed sufficiently in business. Many of the tools to make those changes are in the pages of this book. Some of them may seem very simple – do not be fooled – these exercises will have a profound and far-reaching effect you can't imagine in many areas of your life. And when you complete the activities and exercises in this book, you will recover your respect and high regard for yourself. You will develop a strong and exquisitely feminine sense of yourself as someone of value, of someone with a rightful place and a valuable contribution to make to your own life, your family, your work, your community, your world. You'll grow in self-esteem, valuable beyond belief, and enjoy the freedom to express who you are and who you are meant to be.

How Your Mind Works

Have you ever wondered why you can't stick to your New Year's resolutions no matter how hard you try? Within weeks, you've reverted to old habits, you're discouraged, and probably giving yourself a hard time for failing yet again, feeling powerless because that same old problem keeps cropping up, no matter what you do to try and stop it, or how much you desperately want to change it. Such experiences can leave you with a poor opinion of yourself. And that knocks your self-esteem. Surely if others can do it, why not me?

The answer is simple – it's hard for everyone. We all get stuck trying and trying and not getting anywhere. All that trying builds resistance, and makes it even harder for us to get what we want. Trying, after all, is very trying. It means we have the wrong tools and strategies for the job, and all we do by trying and trying is get better at doing what doesn't work for us. As the wise Yoda says in Star Wars, "There is no try – there is do or not do!"

So please STOP TRYING!

No one finds it easy to make changes to long-established habits, behaviours and beliefs – for good reasons that have to do with how your mind works. Yet, when you begin to work *with* your mind, rather than *against* it, you will find your mind an extremely powerful ally in getting exactly what you want.

So how *does* your mind work? When you understand this, life becomes very fascinating indeed. Although Susie is a Clinical Hypnotherapist and both of us are trained in NLP (neuro-linguistic programming) and Mind Mastery, we're not medical doctors or trained neurologists, so what follows is our simplified lay-woman's version of how the mind works, and how you can work with it to build your self-esteem.

Psychologists make a distinction between the conscious and unconscious mind. Each has a very different role to play in our behaviour, our learning and our beliefs. The conscious mind only accounts for about 1% – 5% of our mind. Typically it evaluates and analyses 40 stimuli per second, and it's the actively creative part, the centre associated with thinking, planning and decision-making, which allows us to observe our own behaviours and emotions and evaluate them. It is here that our desire to change our unwanted behaviours arises. We use the conscious mind to see the past and envision the future. When you understand how to do so, the conscious mind can access the information stored in the unconscious mind and can use that to shape the experiences you want for yourself.

The unconscious mind is vast by comparison and accounts for 95% of our mind – some scientists even say 99%! It can process over 2 million stimuli per second, and react in a split second in order to keep us safe and ensure our survival. It is hard-wired from an early age, even before birth, to automatically regulate our heart rate, our breathing, our blood flow, our digestion and all the other miraculous functions of our body. Yet our mind is not just in our brain – each of our cells is like a hologram and contains a blueprint of the rest of our body. Each cell in our body has its own intelligence and memory, and even though our cells are renewed every 7 years (some are renewed in a matter of days or weeks) cells pass on their stored information like photocopies.

Designed to learn rapidly and create automatic responses to stimuli in our environment, the unconscious mind doesn't know the difference between what is real and what is imaginary, and also is unable to evaluate right or wrong, good or bad. It simply reacts instantaneously with a learned or pre-programmed response, without question. It is like a huge data storage facility, where memories and learned responses are stored for future use.

Because human beings live in complex social environments, learning appropriate reactive strategies and behaviour is essential for survival. So, our brains go to work at a very early age as we take on the attitudes, the fears, beliefs and thinking of our parents in order to survive in the world.

Between birth and the age of six, a child observes her environment very carefully, and copies vast numbers of conditioned responses from her parents and carers into her own system, just like a computer. And they become her truth. Remember though, that their conditioning was passed down to them from their parents, and their parents before them, so our "truth" about ourselves has been passed down to us through the generations from a time totally unrelated to the time in which we live. These early experiences that rule your life are not your own. They are effectively the attitudes, beliefs and opinions of your great-great-grandparents – and are automatically delivered to you spoken in haste, anger or frustration. Chances are they may no longer serve you. This ancestral energy together with our automatic responses, is stored in each and every cell in our bodies.

From a very early age, we look for and expect a response from those around us. If we're met with an emotionless face, we see this as a signal that we're not doing something right and may try and try to get some sort of response. If we fail to connect, which is so important to the female mind, we can so easily lose our positive sense of self, our self-esteem. So what happened when a parent unthinkingly called you a *stupid child* or told you *you don't deserve any better*? Simple. You took it on as absolute truth. Remember, the unconscious mind has no capacity for rational thinking; and you were too young to evaluate it consciously. So in it went, and it continues to affect your behaviour at an unconscious level, hard-wired into your unconscious mind as your truth. Every time a similar stimulus crops up in your life, your unconscious mind instantaneously delivers that learned response, no questions asked.

So, poor self-esteem doesn't mean there's something wrong with you. Lack of self-esteem is purely a reactive behaviour; it's a program you learned as an infant that is still running your life. Because it was learned, it can be unlearned, and new, more life-enhancing behaviours, attitudes and beliefs learned in its stead.

Is it any wonder those New Year's resolutions bite the dust? What you resolve with your conscious mind is often in conflict with how your unconscious mind is programmed to react. And when the conflict arises, the far more powerful unconscious mind wins – it always will.

Unbeknown to you, your body always listens to your mind, responding to every single thought, word, feeling or action, moment to moment. However, your mind seldom listens to your body, and not paying attention to its calls for help can lead to stress and disease. With our tendency at work especially to become more masculine in our behaviour, we are becoming increasingly prone to traditionally male illnesses.

And we are swayed by the way our hormones affect our brain on a daily, even hourly basis. This is not an excuse for behaving badly, nor an excuse for giving up. Rather, this is an opportunity for you to use this understanding and your insights to make a change for the better in your life.

The time has come to change. The process is straightforward, easy and effortless. As you play with the exercises and activities in this book, you will be using the creativity of the conscious mind, the power of the unconscious mind, and your focussed attention to re-program those unwanted behaviour patterns stored in your unconscious mind, so that new, more appropriate behaviours come automatically to you. You already know how to do this, for example when you learn to drive, play a musical instrument or speak another language. This is the process for making desired changes. Here we are simply changing an inappropriate program with one that is more in keeping with who you are, and it can happen easily and quickly. It's fun. It simply requires your attention.

Activities & Exercises

The exercises and activities in this book are straightforward, easy to follow and fun. Many are really simple, and are extremely powerful precisely because of their simplicity. Designed to work the way your mind works, they provide a simple way for your conscious mind to re-program the unconscious mind, correcting old beliefs and deeply-held truths about unworthiness that no longer serve you.

Approach them in a light-hearted and playful way for the best results because they are working at a deep subconscious level to make powerful changes in your physiology, in your biology, in your emotions and mental outlook. They take you through a process whereby you can recover and grow your self-esteem, your self-respect and even self-love.

Often this means simply giving your attention to your feelings or to your situation and going through a particular process that re-programs your mind. Sometimes we ask you to move physically in a way which will help you to unlock earlier patterns, and open you up to creating a new and more empowering way to behave.

We've carefully chosen each exercise to take you through this process, and coded them in all the colours of the rainbow – the colour spectrum of visible light.

The **red** and **orange** zones contain exercises that clear away all unwanted behaviour, and deal with deep-seated fears that are so typical of poor self-esteem – fear of rejection, of being caught out and humiliated. After all, this is how deep-seated beliefs are first installed – in some highly emotional, probably fairly humiliating circumstance that leaves us feeling scarred. The **red** and **orange** zones also deal with poor body image and the crazy way our female hormones seem to rule our life. Constantly seeing the world through these filters tends to reinforce a low opinion of oneself. So, when you can complete these exercises and activities, you'll make significant and lasting changes to how you see yourself and your body. You'll feel so much more comfortable with yourself and you'll be ready to begin to build your self-esteem and self-respect.

The **yellow** and **green** zones give you a new perspective on yourself and on your life. Exercises in the **yellow** zone build your self-esteem and begin to empower you to take charge of your life. Your new found sense of self is delicate however, and so the exercises in the **green** zone teach you how to nurture yourself, and relate to and nurture others around you. They include many powerful processes to replace the old outdated "truths" of not being good enough with new beliefs, new behaviours and perspectives that value who you are, and love and nurture the beautiful woman you are unveiling.

The **blue** and **indigo** zones allow you to further develop and grow your positive self-esteem. They show you how your thoughts affect your sense of self, and how you can change your thinking to maintain your growing self-esteem and self-love. You'll learn how to make decisions that are fully in keeping with who you are becoming. You'll begin to understand and use the power of your mind to create the life you really want.

The **violet** zone is devoted to discovering your vision and purpose so that you can take your new-found sense of self out into the world and make a difference that only you can make. Once you begin to live on purpose, you discover greater meaning in your life as your sense of self strengthens and never fails you. You see why you are here. You realise that every thought you have, every emotion you feel, every word you speak, every action you take makes a positive difference in the world. You have developed a powerful self-respect.

There is an order to these exercises: clear the unwanted beliefs, develop self-esteem and build self-respect. And when you can complete them in order, you will recover your sense of self, and learn to live in ways that are more meaningful to you. You'll discover how to use your mind to make the lasting changes you want – to drop old habits, heal your past, and importantly, replace your old, negative beliefs with ones that nurture and support your growing sense of self. You'll get out of the "stuckness" and discover many ways to eliminate the causes of stress in your life, as you begin to relax and enjoy your new-found confidence.

Simple and easy to follow, these exercises often take less than five minutes to complete. They're set out like a recipe book. At the beginning of each exercise, you'll find a list of the issues it addresses, so that you can quickly turn to the right exercise or activity to do if you've got a particular problem or difficult relationship to handle.

When you can complete them, you'll feel a sense of calm and instant relief. Importantly, you'll discover your exquisite feminine power and restore the balance in your life as you find time to care for yourself as well as others. The rewards at home and at work will exceed your expectations and you may well rekindle the joy, excitement and even the romance in your life.

You'll certainly learn to take charge of your life. You'll feel fulfilled; you'll find purpose and meaning, and get into your flow. You'll discover the great woman you are.

Share your journey with other women who will support you as you support them, because when women come together without fear and in a spirit of co-operation rather than competition, the results are truly magical. As you support and help others develop their self-esteem, your own self-esteem is boosted enormously.

Play with this. Enjoy the journey!

Resources to Draw On

As you begin to play with the activities and exercises in this book, you may be asked to find *"the resources you need right now"*. Resources are anything that may assist you in overcoming your fears, help you let go of past hurts or deep-seated programs, and achieve your goals. And they come in the form of beliefs, values, emotions, or material objects of one kind or another.

> **Tip**
> You don't need years and years of lying on a psychotherapist's couch to gain self-esteem. All you need are the strategies and tools to feel good about yourself, and access to the resources you have inside of you to deal with whatever shows up in your life. You know when you have healthy self-esteem – it's when you feel good about yourself no matter what the external circumstances.

In this short section, we've compiled a list of resources you might find useful. As you do the exercises, you may discover others that are right for you right now. All you have to do is pay attention as you're doing each exercise. The insights will drop into your mind, giving you exactly what you need, when you need it.

Understand that you can only bring a resource to mind if you have known it at some time in your life, however fleeting that moment may have been. So when you're asked – as you will be – to think of a time when you had a particular resource – know that you can recall a time and bring it fully into your experience. If you have difficulty, think of someone you know – or someone in the public eye – who expresses that quality, and imagine you are getting that resource from them.

We've put these resources into balloons – it's a playful way in which we use them throughout the book. Add whatever other resources you need.

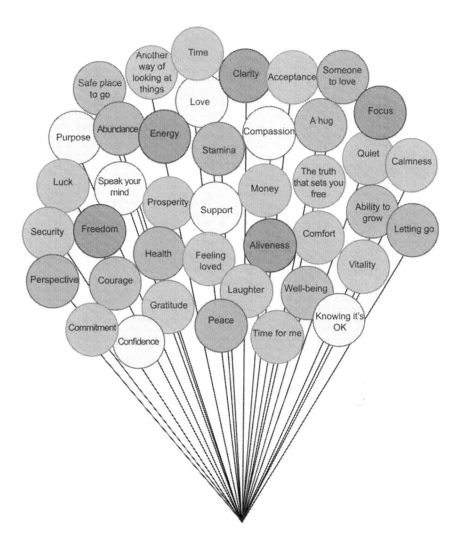

Resources to draw on as you complete the exercises and activities in this book...

The Order of Play

There is an order…to the universe…to our learning…no matter how chaotic it may seem. When we listen, pay attention, things become clear. We are always being shown the way, and it's the right way for us right now. So if you are reading this, just note that this is right for you right now.

There is also an order to this book that will make it easier for you to follow and learn. It is not a random collection of activities and exercises, but a process that makes sense. So we urge you to follow this book in sequence, as it develops your understanding and your growth.

When we first sat down to write this, our writing became stilted and cerebral. When we went on holiday and sat overlooking the mill pond, glistening in the sun, with the swans, cygnets, the head stuff disappeared, and the words came together in perfect order.

This is how life works, when we relax and let it in. When we try too hard, we block the energy and block our flow. As women, we need to give ourselves permission to let go, to let Life flow through us. Intuitively we then get the answers that are right for us.

We're women like you. We've been through it. Remember:

"Life is a game. Which means it has must have rules, and it must be fun. If you don't know the rules, you can't win the game. And if it feels like hard work, your doing the wrong thing."

This is a book of games to make your life fun and meaningful again. You had this once, when you were young. Now is your opportunity to regain that sense of joy and wonder, and really live fully again. To play the game, you need to take action. Play with this. Enjoy the game.

Chapter 1

Rescue Me!

Chapter 1   Rescue Me!

Are you overstretched?
Do you ever feel worried, anxious, or unsure of yourself?
Do you hold yourself back because you're afraid of what others
might think, afraid of being rejected?
Are you stuck in a rut, not knowing what to do to get out –
wondering what's wrong with you and
kicking yourself for being so stupid?
Do you ever panic over unpaid bills or
worry where the money's going to come from?
Do you wonder how other people seem to manage, but not you?

If you've said *"Yes"* to any of these questions, you're operating in survival mode. Yes, you read correctly. You're in survival mode; what we call the **red zone**.

Survival, you ask? Surely survival is not an issue? Let's face it, most of us have enough to eat, a roof over our heads, and sufficient warmth and comfort to keep ourselves and our children alive. But often what we lack is the inner security that makes us feel safe in our environments, both at work and at home; and without this feeling of safety, we cannot grow or develop. *We cannot begin to build healthy self-esteem until we feel safe.* And that means understanding and breaking a few long-standing behaviours and attitudes that keep us locked in fear and stress. This is what the **red zone** is about.

Red is the colour of fear, anxiety and anger. When you use the **red zone** tools, you will release your fears, particularly your fears of rejection and not having enough money. Only then can you begin to feel safe and secure again.

Red is the colour of our connection to the earth and of belonging – to our family, community and country – to our tribe. We learned all about survival from our parents and family, unthinkingly taking on their strategies for coping with the complex world in which they found themselves. Instead of making it easy for us to cope in our own life, these behaviours, attitudes and values can hold us back. They are the

3

ties that bind us to past rules that may no longer be relevant. When you complete the **red zone** activities, you'll re-connect with your true self and your work right now, and build a more compassionate attitude to your family.

Women today are under tremendous pressures at work and at home, and this inevitably leads to stress. Interestingly, we respond to stress very differently from men. We're more sensitive for one thing, because the stress centres in the pre-frontal cortex of our brain are more highly developed, and respond not only to stressors in our external environment, but also to the cyclic rise and fall of oestrogen and progesterone during our monthly cycles. These stress centres react to mental, emotional and physical threats in our environment. (By contrast, a man's stress centres respond only to threats to physical safety.)

It's little wonder then, that we can see a stack of unpaid bills as a massive threat to our survival. Lack of money can be a big problem. It pushes all the wrong buttons and we panic because our safety, our security, our very survival is in jeopardy. Yet the men in our lives can't understand why we're freaking out!

The conflict that arises in such a situation can leave you wondering what's wrong with you, and further damage your self-esteem. You take his comments to heart, and wonder why you're being so emotional, why you're weak and over-sensitive, why you're reacting totally out of hand.

Know that you're not. You're being a woman under stress. That's all. Susie knows this problem only too well. She grew up with conflicting attitudes about money. From her father's family, she learned that money was scarce. Her father's Welsh mining community was rich in voice and poor in pocket; from her mother, she learned something different – that money was attainable if you worked really hard for it. Her maternal ancestors had been pioneers, entrepreneurs and financiers, yet she picked up the scarcity mentality of her father. Whenever her income dropped below a certain level, she'd panic – to the point where she'd be worried, stressed out and feel hopeless and helpless for days at a stretch. When she began to do the money exercises and games in this chapter, she learned to take charge of her money, and no longer see it as a threat. It was something she knew she could handle, and her money anxieties became a thing of her past.

That's why we've included a couple of money exercises here as well as activities to boost your energy when you're exhausted. You'll also find ways of dealing with some of the negative beliefs and attitudes you picked up at an early age.

We assure you, when you can complete the exercises in this chapter, you will cut the ties that bind you to old habits – habits that keep you stuck in reactive behaviour, habits you want to kick because you know they're no longer appropriate.

1. You'll discover how to take charge of your money and spending, and release your money fears and anxieties. In fact, you'll come to feel good about money; you'll see it as a powerful resource in your life, there to support you and your loved ones as you grow and develop.

2. You'll discover the joy of smiling, and how this simple pleasure can take years off your face, restore a wonderful sense of well-being and nurture your self-esteem.

3. You'll learn how to create a safe place where you are always protected, a place where you can nurture yourself and grow your self-esteem.

1   Metallic Catsuit

This powerful little exercise makes you feel safe and keeps you secure, whatever your situation. Turn to it:

If you work in a stressful environment
If you find yourself feeling vulnerable or exposed
When you know you are going into a stressful situation
Where you feel you need some additional support

All you need do to feel safe and secure is, in your imagination, put on your own very special, light-weight, invisible metallic catsuit. This covers you from head to toe and fits you like a glove. Imagine this: not only does it make you look and feel terrific, it renders you with special catlike powers – feminine strength, flexibility, powerful instinct and the ability to relax completely. It's made of light-weight, extremely durable material.

It's selectively sensitive to your experiences, your thoughts and feelings. Good experiences, good thoughts and good feelings can pass through, while negative experiences, thoughts or feelings simply bounce off the reflective surface. Once you have your metallic catsuit on, you're safe; you're protected.

When you can do this exercise first thing in the morning before you start your working day, or before you go into a challenging meeting, then you will immediately notice the benefits. You'll feel more comfortable and self-assured, and whatever is thrown your way, you'll know you are safe and protected. You'll soon realise that even if someone does throw "stuff" at you, you don't have to catch it! Just let it bounce off.

Time Taken: 2 – 3 minutes

1. Imagine you have your metallic catsuit in your hands. It's an invisible one-piece body-stocking that covers you from the tip of your toes to the top of your head, like Cat Woman's costume. Put your feet into it and pull it up over your legs and hips and over your stomach. Put your arms into each sleeve, and pull the suit up over your shoulders and zip it right up to your chin. Pull the

hood up over your hair and fasten it around your chin. You are now ready for whatever the day might throw at you.

2. Your metallic catsuit fits you like a second skin. Whenever you wear it, you look and feel great. You are invincible; you have the courage to speak up for yourself and ask for what you want, because you know your catsuit protects you from all harm – any physical jibes, criticism, harsh words, scathing or unjust remarks bounce off it without harming you in any way.

3. Wear it daily.

This lifts your mood, boosts your energy, tones your face, and nurtures and pampers you. Turn to it:

> *When you look at yourself in the mirror and*
> *all you see are your faults...*
> *If you feel down and need a pick-me-up*
> *Whenever you're giving yourself a hard time*
> *If you're ever in a bad mood*
> *When you feel off-balance*

You step back into your feminine whenever you do this exercise. It is here, in our feminine, that our confidence and self-esteem really lies.

When you make a habit of this every day, your mood at work and at home will begin to shift immediately. You'll think more clearly, have more energy, and find that your relationships improve dramatically. You'll also tone your face and smooth out those worry lines. It's simple:

Time Taken: Less than 2 minutes

1. Smile!

2. Be mindful when you are putting on your cream or make-up. Instead of slapping it on, take time to smooth your creams into your skin. Touch your face, massage it gently and caringly. Smile at your reflection in the mirror.

3. Drop the criticism! Just for this moment, forget the bags under your eyes, your wrinkles or spots. Just don't focus any attention on them. You don't need to buy into the "only the young are beautiful" myth. That's just a ploy to entice you to buy yet another cream, shampoo or beauty product. You are beautiful as you are. Take a few moments each morning to appreciate yourself. And SMILE!

4. Whenever you use the bathroom, smile at yourself in the mirror as you wash your hands. Enjoy the warmth of the water, the scent of the soap. Pamper yourself!

5. Make a conscious effort to smile before you pick up the phone – (people can sense your mood down the telephone, and will respond far better if they sense you are in a good frame of mind) and when you talk to others.

6. Before you know it, this habit will become unconscious. You'll begin to smile easily in any conversation, and others will respond to you by smiling back; because we're wired to respond instinctively like for like, facial expressions are contagious, so putting on a happy face causes those around us to smile.

3   Help! It's Morning!

This exercise is a great way to give yourself an energy boost *before you get out of bed* in the morning. Turn to it:

> *If you wake feeling dull and listless*
> *If you've had a restless night*
> *If you dread the thought of getting out of bed*

The more you feel you're not good enough, or clever enough, or whatever, the more likely you are to feel exhausted. You may not sleep well as a result, and feel that morning comes far too soon. The alarm goes off and all you want to do is roll over and bury your head under the pillow. Yet you know you have to get up and somehow find the energy you need to deal with another day.

This simple exercise boosts your physical energy and improves your mood *before* you get out of bed. It works by stimulating your energy nodes, or acupuncture points, unblocking any jams and allowing your energy to flow naturally. Acupuncture points are tiny spots on the body which the ancient Chinese discovered were keys to locking or unlocking your energy. This exercise focuses on those located around the ear and the thymus.

When you remember to do this before you get out of bed, you'll get up relaxed and refreshed, with the energy you need to greet a new day. It's also great to do whenever you need an energy pick-me-up during the day.

Time Taken: less than 1 minute

1. While still lying in bed, tug around your ears, gently pulling the ear lobes, and massaging around the whole of the external ear. You'll be surprised just how sensitive the ears are.

2. Stretch your arms and legs fully as you take three deep breaths.

3. Put your fist on your breast bone and repeatedly tap it firmly for about 20 seconds as you breathe deeply. This stimulates the

thymus to produce infection-fighting hormones which guard your health and keep you strong.

4.   Get out of bed, with a firm intention of having a great day.

This encourages you to overcome your fears of money and begin to use it wisely in your life. Turn to it:

*When a bill comes through the letter box and
you wish it would go away
When the bills and bank statements pile up, unopened
When even the thought of money brings you out in a panic
When you really can't face your money problems*

Do you find it hard to open your bank statement or credit card bill? Do you look at the envelope and know exactly what it is the moment it arrives, yet dread opening it up? Do you have bills that sit unopened for weeks or even months at a stretch? What thoughts run through your head when a bill or bank statement arrives? Are you fearful? Do you worry about how you're going to pay the bill? Do you feel threatened or insecure? Or is it all too much to handle? You just want it to go away.

Don't worry, you're not alone. We've met hundreds of people who do this, but let's have a look and see what we can do instead.

This is such a common experience, especially for women, because our minds are wired to panic if our security and that of our loved ones is threatened in any way. We associate money with security, because it provides for our basic physical needs. It's little wonder that an unwanted bill is seen as a huge threat to our well-being – indeed, even our survival!

Do you know that your wealth is in your words? Wealth lies in the language you use to express yourself, as each and every word we use and the tonality in which we use them affect our unconscious mind – we will explain more in the **blue zone** of this book. Very often the words we use out of habit aren't ours anyway. They are automatic responses to situations which we have learned from our parents as we were growing up; so our attitude towards money problems is often inherited from our parents' parents' parents' parents, which means they are mostly irrelevant to our 21st century experience. You can give them up any time you choose.

We are not suggesting that you be irresponsible with money; we just want to help you see where the fear and anxiety about money stems from. So, when you can play this game every time a bill or bank statement arrives in the mail, you'll overcome your fear, and see it for what it really is – a communication from your bank or lender – nothing more, nothing less. It is *You* that gives it meaning.

You'll come to appreciate the accuracy of that financial information and use it to handle your money in ways that are more in keeping with who you are and what you value. You'll realise that your lenders are generous – they've let you have all those goods and services you've bought for free. It's only now, after 4 or 6 weeks, that they're asking you to pay up.

You'll discover that money is a game with numbers; it's easy and fun to play once you know the rules. You'll learn to drop your knee-jerk reaction to money, and feel more comfortable handling it, spending, saving and investing it for your benefit and the benefit of those you love.

Time Taken: No more than 5 minutes

1. Gather up all your unopened bills and bank statements and place them in a grand pile in the centre of a table.

2. Stand up. Pretend that you're the MC at the Oscars. Imagine you're dressed to the hilt in an exquisite evening gown that makes you look and feel terrific. It's your job to announce the awards for best actor, best actress, best screenplay, best supporting actor and actress, best sound track...

3. Pick up the first unopened bill with a flourish and announce the first winner. Imagine the fanfare as you rip open the letter with excitement.
   "And the winner is..."

4. Open the letter. Look at it without reading it all the way through. It's just information – numbers on a sheet of paper. Announce the winner.

   "Master Card for the grand sum of ...."

5. Thank the Oscar committee, your mum and dad, grandparents, your bank, all the people who made this possible. Really ham it up!

6. Start two more piles on the table – one for opened bills and one for statements from banks, building societies, and investment funds.

7. Pick up the next unopened envelope and repeat the exercise with great flourish… *"The winner is…"* and place it on one of the opened piles.

8. This is a time to celebrate, because you've already had the use of these goods and services – gas, electricity, new shoes, dinner at a nice restaurant, theatre trip, etc.

9. If you feel happy and comfortable paying these bills now, do so, and really be grateful for what you've already enjoyed at someone else's expense.

10. If the thought of paying your bills overwhelms you right now, there's an exercise to help you on the next page.

5   Debt Buster

Debt can weigh us down and leave our self-esteem in tatters. This exercise empowers you to confront your debt. Turn to it:

If you feel your debt is out of hand
If you feel helpless or hopeless about facing your money problems
When you need help to put your money situation into perspective

When you can do this exercise, you'll understand your attitude to debt and be in a position to take charge of it. You'll never feel helpless or hopeless again. In fact, your relationship to debt and to money will change for the better forever.

However, you do need to be calm before you can get the most out of this activity – not in a state of panic over those unpaid bills. If you are, then take half a dozen deep breaths to relax before you begin.

During this exercise, you will get three different perspectives on your debt. Initially, you'll experience it from your current perspective – with all the thoughts, worries, concerns and feelings you have about it right now. This is the money box in which you live right now. The good thing about this box is that it has transparent walls and no lid, so if you feel stuck there, understand and remember you can step out of it whenever you choose.

When you do step out, you'll be guided to move physically to take on a second perspective where you'll stand right in the middle of your debt. From this perspective, you'll probably acknowledge it fully and own it for the first time. Remember there are financial professionals who deal with people like you every day, people who have problems in paying off their loans or credit card debt. The professionals can – and do – provide lots of options that make it easy for you to clear your debt in a way and at a level that is comfortable and workable for you. It's in their interest to help you. From this position, you'll gain valuable insights into how you can approach them, and deal with your debt.

Finally, you'll move physically to a position of great resourcefulness. From this position, you can see yourself in your box with all your worries and concerns about money, and also your mound of debt. In this place you are open to any and all the resources you need to handle your debt in a way that is fully in keeping with who you are and what you value. In this position, you'll be given all the resources you need.

Taking all these resources with you, you can then step back into your money box, and realise exactly what you need to do to handle your debt easily and effortlessly. Feeling really empowered, you can push the walls of the box down as you are no longer stuck.

This is a powerful exercise, because it gives you perspective and exactly the resources you need.

Time Taken: 15 to 20 minutes

1. Find a place where you will not be disturbed. You will need sufficient space in which to place three mats on the floor as illustrated below.

2. Go to position 1. Here you are standing opposite your debt, with all the worry and stress that is placing on you. In this position, really experience what it is like to have this debt. What do you see? What do you hear? What do you feel?

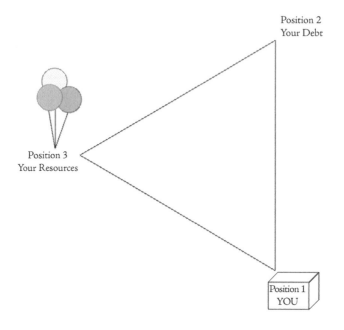

16

3. What thoughts, feelings and insights do you have? Make a note of them.

4. Remember, your box at position 1 has transparent walls and no lid. You can step out of it whenever you like.

5. When you're ready, step out of position 1 and shake yourself off. Giving yourself a really good physical shake out makes sure you leave all your thoughts, worries and feelings about debt on the floor at position 1.

6. When you've shaken off those feelings, step into your debt at position 2. See what it's like to be on the other side, owning your debt and your debt problems.

7. See what you see; hear what you hear; feel what you feel. Really experience what it's like to be in debt. Take time to discover what thoughts, feelings and insights you have from this position.

8. Shake yourself off, and then move to position 3, where you are open to receive all the resources you need to deal with this problem. In this position, you can see yourself at position 1, your debt at position 2, and the way you interact with it and it with you.

9. What resources do you need at position 1 in order to deal with your debt? (You can use the resource balloons in Resources to get you started.) Make a note of what is needed, as these insights reveal themselves to you. You don't need to force anything; the right answers will come to you.

10. If you find it difficult to find the resources you need, put a chair at position 3 and step up onto it to give yourself a new perspective.

11. Once you've discovered what resources you need, be open to receive them. Call out the first resource and imagine a brightly

coloured cloak full of that resource floating down to you. Put it on and then call out for the next.

12. Imagine this next resource will float down to you as a magic amulet or bracelet to protect and guide you. Physically act out putting it on your wrist, and ask for the other resources you need. These may come as other pieces of clothing, as make-up, or jewellery; use the power of your imagination to guide you. Take each resource and put it on. You'll feel protected, comfortable and ready to face your debt.

13. Wearing all these wonderful resources, step back into position 1. Experience what it's like to confront your debt with *exactly what you need*. What do you see, hear and feel as you face your debt, knowing exactly what to do?

14. Experience the power and the confidence that this gives you.

15. Check that your resourceful approach really will work with your debt. Shake yourself off. Move to position 2. From here, you can experience what it's like to deal with this far more resourceful, empowered woman who's ready and willing to handle her debt.

16. If you feel really comfortable, take what you have learned and use it to handle your debt far more effectively and more in keeping with who you are and what you value.

17. If there are any unresolved issues that arise, run through positions 3, then 1 and 2 again.

18. Enjoy feeling really comfortable with money – and with debt. They're both powerful allies on your route to wealth.

Being untidy can really knock your self-esteem. The clutter gets to you after a while. Turn to this fun game:

When your clutter is getting out of hand and starting to bug you
When you've allowed all those bills and papers to pile up
When you have so much stuff around you're tripping over it

One of our greatest fears as women is that we will end up on the streets living out of a bag – being a bag lady! So in this exercise, we give ourselves permission, just for a short time, to play being a bag lady.

Do this exercise if you are untidy, and have things scattered all over the floor. This is particularly useful if you have lots of papers you haven't yet filed, or don't quite know what to do with yet, and is very useful after you have paid your bills. Do this in 20 minute time slots so it is always fresh and fun to do.

Time Taken: No more than 20 minutes

1. Find a pretty bag – our local supermarkets now sell Bags for Life, which are plastic shopping bags with lovely designs on front and back

2. Put all your papers, bills, bits and pieces, anything that's lying around on your floor, on your desk, tables, etc., into the bag or bags.

3. Put some music on that really inspires you, something you can sing along to.

4. Put your hand in the bag and do a lucky dip – pull one piece of paper or one object out of the bag. It's like Christmas because you have no idea what you are taking out until you look at it.

Keep breathing

5. Now look at what is in your hand and deal with it – either file it, or put it away or bin it if it is no longer needed.

6. Hurrah! Now put your hand in the bag again for another lucky dip. Keep this up for no more than 20 minutes at a stretch.

7. Make clearing your clutter something to look forward to.

Chapter 2

Orange Pips

Chapter 2   Orange Pips

Do you feel mortified whenever anyone criticizes you?
Are you edgy, irritable and in pain at your time of the month,
wondering why you can't cope when other women seem to be able to?
Do you find it hard to cope with all the problems you have?
Are other people pushing you around, wasting your time and energy?
Do you find it hard to say No?
Are you always on the go, exhausted and irritable?

If so, you're in the **orange zone**, finding it hard to cope, feeling hurt and betrayed by another's cutting remarks, struggling to set and keep boundaries in your relationships at home and at work – and failing to recognize the importance of moving in time to the natural rhythms of your body.

Often, we're so stretched we don't take time to appreciate who we are. We spend all day at work, only to come home and immediately assume our other jobs without a break. Relationships can't help but be strained. Finding it hard to focus, fatigued, irritable, stressed, overworked and seldom really appreciated for all the good that you do, you can easily lose your cool. Add to this mix the potent cocktail of hormones that constantly fluctuates in your body and it's little wonder you break down, or lash out at someone close to you.

And if all you're doing is coping at best, your self-esteem suffers. So what you need to do is stop right now and discover better coping strategies so that you can find the time and space to build healthy self-esteem. That's what the **orange zone** is all about.

> **Tip**
> Almira had a coaching client who was struggling to cope with her home and work commitments. When she worked through all her to-do lists, she discovered she had 56 different roles. It's little wonder she couldn't cope! Deciding which ones mattered to her, which ones she could delegate and which she could simply drop was a major breakthrough for her.

Orange is the colour of our boundaries. It is the colour of enthusiasm, warm-heartedness, self-sufficiency and confidence. When you complete the **orange zone** exercises, you'll know how to say "No" to what you don't want, and "Yes" to what you do; you'll know how to deal with criticism in ways that empower rather than hurt you; you'll learn to deal with your problems in more creative and resourceful ways. You'll find many tools in the **orange zone** to restore your confidence, and make you more compassionate and respectful in your dealings with others.

Often we fail to recognize, acknowledge and respect the natural rhythms of our bodies. We may not even appreciate what is going on. Yet every day of your menstrual cycle, you have a different brain – a brain that is bathed in a potent mix of oestrogen and progesterone as well as other feel-good – or feel-lousy – hormones. In the early part of the cycle, oestrogen, (the feel-great hormone) is high, and you're probably feeling confident, focused, and very much in charge. Give yourself a couple of weeks though, and oestrogen falls and you feel the calming effects of rising progesterone. Then the killer hits; just a few days before your period, both oestrogen and progesterone fall off dramatically, and all hell is let loose.

Around 90 per cent of menstruating women get advance warning of an approaching period because of physical and/or psychological changes in the days before their period begins. For most women the symptoms are mild, but a small proportion finds their symptoms so severe that they dread this time of the month. The terms "mild" and "severe" in respect of PMS are arbitrary, but relate to the extent of disruption to your home and work life that's attributable to the monthly cycle. You may find it hard to focus, you may become irritable; you may even suffer migraines, pre-menstrual cramps, or tension. It's a time to rest, to nurture and nourish your body.

We found out that when we nourish our body with life-giving foods and high quality supplements, with appropriate exercise and rest, our minds become much clearer and our bodies supple and strong and able to deal with life in a far better way than before. There are rhythms to all of life. We see it in the seasons, in the phases of the moon by which we as women are particularly affected. And for all women, there is a time to be active and a time to rest. There must always be time to respect who we are and to value our monthly rhythms as a wonderful part of our nature, as the seat of our creativity and healthy sexuality.

So often, that value and respect are missing. Those around us fail to give it to us, because so often, we fail to give it to ourselves. Despite the fact that there are some very derogatory terms for our natural cycles and body parts, it's important we don't denigrate our menstrual cycles and intimate relationships by using them ourselves. Such words come to define who we are as women. (For more on how language defines our reality, see the **blue** and **indigo** zones.) Whenever you hear derogatory words or use them, you pull yourself down. In fact, such words pull all women down. They lower your self-esteem and the self-esteem of all women. An important part of healthy self-esteem is lifting someone else's self-esteem, because when we do this we automatically improve our own.

When you can complete all the activities and exercises in this chapter, you'll feel much more comfortable in your body. You'll accept the natural rhythms of being a woman, and discover how easily you can deal with the inevitable ups and downs, the ebb and flow of your energy and emotions.

1. You'll learn how to handle problems and difficult situations. In fact, you'll transform those situations so that they become a source of joy and fulfilment for you and others concerned.

2. You'll discover how to deal with criticism in a way that uplifts you, rather than pulls you down. You'll actually feel good afterwards – in charge of your feelings and your response to any potentially hurtful remarks.

3. You'll learn to set boundaries for yourself and accept them in others. Respecting another's boundaries and having other people accept and respect yours allow you to regain your self-sufficiency. It gives you the protection and support you need as you begin to uncover and nurture your healthy self-esteem.

4. You'll learn how to say "No" – "No" to demands on your time and energy, "No" to situations that leave you weak and powerless – and enjoy the power and freedom this gives you.

5. You'll re-connect with your exquisitely feminine creativity, and your natural feminine talents for relating to other people. Importantly, you'll learn how to control the dynamics of your outer environment – with those in authority and with other people. You'll learn to trust your instincts. You'll feel in control.

This is a brilliant way to control – or eliminate – your pain without the need for any painkillers. Use it:

If you suffer from a headache or migraine
If your pre-menstrual or menstrual pain is too much for you
If you suffer lower back pain

Pain is a signal. It's feedback from your body about your body, about what is not working in your life. This activity helps you to respect it and acknowledge it for the important lessons it brings you.

Having said that, there are times when you hurt. These may be pre-menstrual cramps, migraine headaches, or the sharp stab in your lower back that crops up whenever you feel you're not getting the help you need.

Migraines and pre-menstrual cramps can be so painful they stop you in your tracks. You're irritable and snap at anyone who comes near you. And feel bad because you didn't mean it. You'd like to hide it from men – especially male colleagues – who don't understand what's going on. You may even feel that other women who don't suffer from this are judging you.

Instead of reaching for a pain-killer to ease the symptoms, why not try this gentler, drug-free approach to easing your pain? Because it works on the problem, not the symptoms, it is very effective.

Pain in any part of your body is a gift. Your body is sending you an alarm signal that something is seriously amiss, and the location of the pain is the source of that problem. If you pay attention to it, rather than drug it, you are on your way to reducing the pain, and eliminating the source of it from your life. All you need to do is pay attention to it, and play with it. That's the power of this exercise.

When you can complete this activity, you'll acknowledge yourself and your pain, and bring your migraine, your PMS cramps or back pain under control. In fact, you'll learn a lot about the quality of this pain, where it affects you and how it affects you. And you'll discover a simple way to alleviate pain, improve your mood and restore balance. You'll feel sane and normal again.

1. Sit comfortably in a chair, with your feet flat on the floor, and your hands upturned on your lap

2. Close your eyes and begin to breathe deeply and gently through your nose, into your belly and up into your lungs, keeping your shoulders soft and relaxed

3. Now pay attention to your pain.

4. Where exactly do you feel it? Please don't let this question confuse you. We're asking you to pay close attention to the pain, and discover exactly where in your body you feel that pain. Take your time. Be as specific as you can in locating the source of your pain.

5. What does it feel like? Describe as accurately as you can the *quality* of the pain. Is it a dull ache? Does it throb or pound? If so, how fast is it throbbing? Is it sharp and stabbing? How intense is the pain? You may find that simply by paying attention to your pain and acknowledging it, it recedes.

6. Once you have identified where the pain is, and what quality is has, begin to play with it. Imagine you have a dial in your hand which controls the intensity, like a volume control. Now turn up that intensity, that volume. Keep making it more intense until you really can't bear it. Now turn it down again.

7. Change its quality. If it's dull and aching, make it pound. Is this better or worse? Make it pound faster and faster; now slow it down to the point where it stops. Start it throbbing again; make it louder and louder, then softer and softer. If it's throbbing, turn it into a stabbing pain. Again, play with the volume or intensity of the pain, turning it up and down at will. Discover from this process what feels best for you – a light dull ache, a slowly throbbing pain, or some other configuration you've tried.

8. Once you've played with the quality of the pain, begin to shift it around, from one part of your body to another. Play with the intensity and quality as you do so. Keep playing like this until you really feel that you're in charge of your pain. In the process you'll discover that certain qualities of pain feel better than others; in certain parts of your body, the pain will feel better than in others.

9. Once you feel you are in control, swap it to the most "comfortable" pain you've experienced, and ask yourself if you are able to live with it like this. If so, complete this exercise by opening your eyes. Say thank you to your body and mind for being able to control your pain.

10. If not, move the pain to another part of your body where it least bothers you – down your right arm, or into your left big toe. Leave it there, or if you wish, move it to one of your fingers and then place that finger on a table or chair, your desk, some object in your environment, and gently leave it there. You can come back and pick it up anytime you like.

11. Once you're complete, open your eyes, say thank you to your body and carry on with your day.

This is one of two exercises to help you deal with hurtful criticism. Use it:

If someone is criticizing you

When someone is criticizing you, it's easy to take their words to heart; and when you do that, your self-esteem suffers yet another blow. Because criticism is hurtful or scary, you tend not to listen, thinking you're protecting yourself. Even so, the words go deep inside and fester. You begin to believe that's who you are, without realising it's only someone's opinion of you, and they may be wrong.

When you can remember to do this the next time someone criticizes you, you'll stop the critic in his or her tracks. You'll discover you do have a choice – and the power to deal with criticism differently. You'll realise that their words are not a reflection of you, but of them – merely an expression of *what is wrong with you in their eyes*. In time, you'll discover that your critics really haven't anything negative or hurtful to say to you any more. They'll realise that their remarks don't affect you and they'll stop.

Time Taken: less than 1 minute

1. When someone criticizes you, give them your absolute full attention, with no defensiveness. Don't be concerned about what to say next.

2. Just look them straight in the eyes and let them spit it out.

3. Thank them for letting you know what *they think is wrong with you*. This will almost certainly throw them! They won't know how to reply.

4. Turn and walk away.

Adding Spice
9 And Your Point Is? in the **orange zone** on the next page.

9 And Your Point is?

This exercise helps you turn around those situations:

If someone is criticizing you unfairly
If someone makes a hurtful remark about you or to you

When someone makes an unjust remark about us, it may be hard to keep it from getting personal, and hurting us deeply. We tend to believe what people are telling us, without realising it's just their opinion. If you know what they are saying simply is not true, instead of getting defensive, here's a simple solution. In fact, when you can remember to do this exercise at the time, you'll quickly turn the situation around, so that you are very much in charge. Do it repeatedly, and before long, you'll find that you simply don't take anyone's hurtful comments to heart – you can't. You've changed your mind.

This exercise is not about having you throw your weight around. Rather it encourages you to be calm and not let painful emotions get the better of you.

Time Taken: less than 1 minute

1. If someone says something unfair or hurtful about you, imagine that the person making this remark is drunk and slurring his or her words, tripping over his feet, staggering about.

2. It all sounds stupid and looks ridiculous. Smile!

3. If they're going on and on and you can't get a word in edgeways, say simply and dispassionately *"And your point is?"*

4. This is likely to confuse them – scramble their brain because they're not expecting such a response.

5. Smile, and walk away.

10   Just Say "STOP!"

This exercise shows you how to deal with people who drain your energy. Turn to it:

> *If you're bored with someone who is droning*
> *on and on about ... nothing*
> *If you're being nice to someone who is griping or groaning*
> *If you're caught up in an endless discussion about*
> *someone's illness or problems*
> *If ever you're with someone who is draining your energy*
> *If someone is trying your patience*

As women, we tend to connect with others more easily than men do. We're natural communicators, able to listen for and pick up the subtle emotional nuances in a person's face and voice. We read others' feelings and moods quickly and accurately. We love to talk, to communicate, and find it easy to express our feelings more freely than men. It's how we are programmed to deal with our world. Connecting with other people is essential to our well-being and our fulfilment. The more deeply we connect, the more fulfilled we become.

There are four levels at which we can communicate with others. We spend most of our time at the lowest level, *exchanging* facts, information and complaints. This is the level of coffee-machine banter, office gossip, complaining about anything we can complain about, or worrying about what is going on in the world.

At the next level, we *connect* with others. We reach out and touch their hearts; we move them with our words, our concern, our respect or our love. Beyond connecting, we *motivate* and *inspire*.

Whilst it's really easy – and important – for us to connect, there are times when it can drag us down. Because of our need to connect, we tend to empathise with the people around us, so we don't feel left out – we feel we belong. When you find yourself deeply involved with moaners and complainers and when you're around women who focus on illness or myriad problems in their lives, you begin to absorb their negativity and their low energy, and your own energy drops. You can get hypnotised by their negativity.

When you can complete this exercise any time you're with the moaners and groaners in your life, you'll immediately raise your energy levels as well as theirs. You'll appreciate your growing power to set boundaries for yourself as to what is acceptable to you and what isn't. And you'll quieten the moaners in your life – whether it's your own internal "moaning Minnie" or others.

Time Taken: less than 1 minute

1. If ever you're with someone – or a group of people – who are complaining, moaning and going on and on about lots of negative "stuff" that drags you down and makes you feel awful, simply say *"STOP!"* Say it nicely, say it with compassion. Just say *"STOP!"*

2. Your companions will almost certainly wake up from their hypnosis. Again, simply say *"STOP!"*

3. Let them know gently and firmly that you simply don't want to talk about that subject any more. Talking about some terrible disaster or another doesn't help that situation. In fact it gives the misery more energy – and in turn depletes your own energy. When we feel helpless or powerless to do something, our self-esteem takes a nose-dive. When you let the topic go, it no longer has an emotional or energetic hold on you.

4. Ask instead what you can focus on that makes you feel healthy, strong, vital and alive. Your companions will thank you for it.

5. You have another choice here: if there is a disaster, rather than just worry about it or gossip about it, go and do something useful towards alleviating the suffering. Find out what is most needed and contribute – time, money, goods. It will help a worthy cause and contribute so much more value than just talking about it, and in turn will raise your self-esteem.

11   Name it. Shame it!

Your feelings and mood may fluctuate over the course of the day and week. Some feelings uplift you, while others make you feel really bad. This powerful little activity makes you aware of – and really puts paid to – all those bad feelings you have. Use it:

> *If you feel angry, hurt or resentful*
> *If you feel bored, dull or unresponsive*
> *If you are jealous, or envious of others*
> *If ever you give yourself a hard time over something you said or did*
> *In short, if ever you feel bad*

This is a little game to play if ever you feel bad, or start to give yourself a hard time over something you've said or done (or not said or not done). As you play this game, remember that you do not need to get involved in the feelings. If you do, you bring that bad energy into your body, and that's what makes your skin wrinkly and your bottom sag! Change is an inside job. So instead, simply acknowledge your bad feelings and let them go.

When you can remember to play this game if ever you feel down for any reason whatsoever, you'll soon find that your mood shifts for the better. You'll realise you can take charge of your feelings and moods, and that knowledge will bolster your confidence and self-esteem. You will leave your bad thoughts, moods and feelings on the page. And then all you need to do is chuck it out at the end of the day.

Time Taken: A few seconds throughout the day

1. Keep a *'Bad Feelings Register'*.

2. Start a clean register every morning, using a copy of the form overleaf.

3. Whenever you feel frustrated, irritable or angry, just tick the box; do the same for any of the other emotions on the form. Add any other emotions you want to this list.

4. Acknowledge the feeling as your feeling. Once it's on the page, it's no longer in your body. Just say to yourself *"Oh that's interesting, I've just done anger again."* And let it go. Your aim is to have an awareness of these feelings without being attached to them or going into them.

5. As the day goes on, you may feel the same emotion again and again. Just put another tick in the box beside that emotion. It will tell you a lot about where your energy is trapped, and give you insights into where your emotional energy is being spent.

6. At the end of the day, take your *'Bad Feelings Register'*, crumple it up and throw it out. It's gone and so are the bad feelings on it. Good riddance!

Bad Feelings Register

Angry	☐	☐	☐	☐	☐	☐	☐	☐	☐	☐
Annoyed	☐	☐	☐	☐	☐	☐	☐	☐	☐	☐
Anxious	☐	☐	☐	☐	☐	☐	☐	☐	☐	☐
Ashamed	☐	☐	☐	☐	☐	☐	☐	☐	☐	☐
Blaming	☐	☐	☐	☐	☐	☐	☐	☐	☐	☐
Bored	☐	☐	☐	☐	☐	☐	☐	☐	☐	☐
Depressed	☐	☐	☐	☐	☐	☐	☐	☐	☐	☐
Despairing	☐	☐	☐	☐	☐	☐	☐	☐	☐	☐
Devastated	☐	☐	☐	☐	☐	☐	☐	☐	☐	☐
Discouraged	☐	☐	☐	☐	☐	☐	☐	☐	☐	☐
Dumb	☐	☐	☐	☐	☐	☐	☐	☐	☐	☐
Exhausted	☐	☐	☐	☐	☐	☐	☐	☐	☐	☐
Fat	☐	☐	☐	☐	☐	☐	☐	☐	☐	☐
Fearful	☐	☐	☐	☐	☐	☐	☐	☐	☐	☐
Frustrated	☐	☐	☐	☐	☐	☐	☐	☐	☐	☐
Guilty	☐	☐	☐	☐	☐	☐	☐	☐	☐	☐
Helpless	☐	☐	☐	☐	☐	☐	☐	☐	☐	☐
Hopeless	☐	☐	☐	☐	☐	☐	☐	☐	☐	☐
Horrid	☐	☐	☐	☐	☐	☐	☐	☐	☐	☐
Hurt	☐	☐	☐	☐	☐	☐	☐	☐	☐	☐
Impatient	☐	☐	☐	☐	☐	☐	☐	☐	☐	☐
Insecure	☐	☐	☐	☐	☐	☐	☐	☐	☐	☐
Insignificant	☐	☐	☐	☐	☐	☐	☐	☐	☐	☐
Irritated	☐	☐	☐	☐	☐	☐	☐	☐	☐	☐
Jealous	☐	☐	☐	☐	☐	☐	☐	☐	☐	☐
Low	☐	☐	☐	☐	☐	☐	☐	☐	☐	☐
Overwhelmed	☐	☐	☐	☐	☐	☐	☐	☐	☐	☐
Pessimistic	☐	☐	☐	☐	☐	☐	☐	☐	☐	☐
P****d-off	☐	☐	☐	☐	☐	☐	☐	☐	☐	☐

Resentful	☐	☐	☐	☐	☐	☐	☐	☐	☐	☐
Sad	☐	☐	☐	☐	☐	☐	☐	☐	☐	☐
Shattered	☐	☐	☐	☐	☐	☐	☐	☐	☐	☐
Stressed Out	☐	☐	☐	☐	☐	☐	☐	☐	☐	☐
Stuck	☐	☐	☐	☐	☐	☐	☐	☐	☐	☐
Stupid	☐	☐	☐	☐	☐	☐	☐	☐	☐	☐
Thick	☐	☐	☐	☐	☐	☐	☐	☐	☐	☐
Ugly	☐	☐	☐	☐	☐	☐	☐	☐	☐	☐
Unworthy	☐	☐	☐	☐	☐	☐	☐	☐	☐	☐
Upset	☐	☐	☐	☐	☐	☐	☐	☐	☐	☐
Wiped out	☐	☐	☐	☐	☐	☐	☐	☐	☐	☐
Worried	☐	☐	☐	☐	☐	☐	☐	☐	☐	☐

12   Flush It

The beauty of this simple exercise is that you can flush your problems away. Turn to it:

Whenever the pressure at work builds up too much
If you find yourself overburdened with your own – or other
people's problems
If you're worried or anxious
If you feel overwhelmed by all you have to do

Know that when you can complete this simple exercise, you'll flush your worries and problems away. What a relief!

Time Taken: 10 to 15 minutes

1. First collect your resources. You'll need a ball point pen and a single sheet of toilet paper. (Although a fountain pen is even better for putting your problems in perspective)

2. Write down all your problems on this sheet of toilet paper. Cram them in. Write up the sides, on the back, everywhere there is even the tiniest space. Carry on until you've written down everything that troubles or worries you.

3. Take your sheet of toilet paper to the bathroom.

4. Throw it into the toilet bowl, and with great ceremony, flush it away.

5. Wave all your problems and worries good bye as they disappear down the drain!

Please play this game with care. One sheet of toilet paper and a small flush is all you need. The whole roll will block the drains and upset everyone around you!

13   Wand to the Ready!

This simple exercise cures a blunder. Use it:

If ever you put your foot in it
If you say the wrong thing
If you step out of turn …
… and give yourself a hard time about it for hours afterwards

Such behaviour really demolishes your self-esteem. Indeed, when you can remember to do this exercise any time you inadvertently put your foot in it, you'll immediately feel better. In fact, you'll find you are back in charge of your life, and ready for the next experience.

Time Taken: less than 1 minute

1. Imagine you have a magic wand always at the ready. This is a state of the art wand, which sprinkles fairy dust on to any problem or difficult situation and immediately disables it. A little "pop" and the problem has disappeared.

2. When you make a gaffe, recognize it for what it is

3. Acknowledge it, wave your magic wand at it, watch it go "pop" and disappear.

4. Laugh. You never need to feel bad about a gaffe again.

Chapter 3

Me, Myself and I

Chapter 3   Me, Myself and I

In the red and orange zones, you've had the opportunity to clear and improve your energy; you've re-worked early experiences so that they no longer have such an emotional hold over you; you've learned how to handle difficult situations and criticism from those around you.

Now it is time to move on and develop your sense of self, to improve your self- image, to build healthy self-esteem and self-respect.

Do you feel uncomfortable in your body?
Are you too short, too tall, too thin, too fat, too...?
Do you constantly look to others for approval?
Are you self-conscious?
Do you find it hard to speak up for yourself?
Do you feel others are taking advantage of you?
Are you afraid your weaknesses will be found out?
Are you afraid to let your light shine?

If so, you're in the **yellow zone**, grappling with your poor sense of self, concerned about how others see you, possibly to the point where their opinions of you matter more to you than your own. Indeed, your own opinion of yourself may be pretty low.

You may feel uncomfortable about your body, or fear looking foolish in front of others. You may find you still look to others for approval, for permission to be yourself, or to do what you really, really want to do. You may still hide your innermost secrets for fear that others may discover that you can't actually do what they think you can, or haven't got what you think you ought. Or you may be hiding your true talents under a bushel for fear of being regarded as a show-off.

Interestingly enough, these natural fears of the self and self-expression are held by almost everyone, regardless of how successful they appear to be. It is only when you begin to address and overcome them that you will be far more in charge of your true self and your life. You'll begin to take responsibility for what you say and do; you'll build that important bridge to healthy self-esteem and self-respect. That's what the **yellow zone** is all about.

Yellow is the colour of personal power, of self-esteem and self-respect. It is the colour of the ego and the personality. In the **yellow zone** you will find the tools you need to *truly empower yourself, to take charge of your ego and build healthy self-esteem and self-respect.*

Yellow stirs up our fears of looking foolish and reminds us of all those things wrong with our physical appearance, the niggling faults we see whenever we look in the mirror – faults that add up to the poor image we hold of our bodies and ourselves. The exercises and activities in the **yellow zone** teach you to accept, love and appreciate yourself as the beautiful woman you are. Yellow is about your relationship with yourself – and it's expansive.

Remember, you don't learn self-esteem by reading a book. You learn it by changing your mind-set and by taking action, by doing – the activities, the exercises here are structured processes to take you on your path. So when you can follow and complete all the exercises in this chapter, you'll regain your self-esteem. You'll take responsibility for your self and come to accept, to respect and love yourself for who you are.

1. You'll learn to honour yourself, develop your courage and strength of character. You'll know better who you are and what you represent and you'll find it easier to stand up for yourself and your beliefs and values.

2. You'll discover how to deal with the fears that keep you stuck, and keep you constantly asking others for permission to be. You'll learn how to take the power out of any bad experiences you may have had.

3. You'll learn how to heal past hurts and early negative beliefs about yourself, and how to cut your emotional ties to them so that they no longer influence and control your reactions.

4. You'll discover how to handle your internal critic in a way that frees you from her constant disapproval.

5. You'll come to accept, love and appreciate your body. Be prepared to shed tears of sadness and joy as you discover how truly magnificent you are, just the way you are.

6. You'll learn how to change your state – improve your mood – whenever YOU want. No more being the slave to your emotions! You'll always have a powerful exercise up your sleeve to take you from feeling bad to feeling good in a matter of seconds.

7. You'll discover a few of the ways in which you can re-program your mind to eliminate negative patterns and replace them with what you really want. And you will delight in how your unconscious mind will deliver this new pattern automatically to you because that's what it's designed to do.

This powerful exercise re-writes your past, taking all the emotional heat out of an early, possibly traumatic experience that still holds you back. Turn to it:

If you want to cure a phobia – of spiders, heights, open or closed spaces, etc.
If you are afraid of rejection
If you fear looking like a fool, or being caught out
If you don't understand why you stay in a dead-end job or abusive relationship
If you know your fears are holding you back
If you need to ask someone else's permission to be

Such fears add up to low self-esteem. Someone may have said or done something to you in the past that hurt you or took away your power. Maybe you've forgotten it; maybe it's still as vivid and clear as the day you experienced it. You keep playing that experience over and over again in your mind. And with each replay, you feel worse and worse about yourself. You may resent the person who did this to you, and your anger and bitterness only fuel the flame and keep that experience alive and messing up your life.

Now is the time to deal with that episode once and for all. It's a thing of the past, and needs to be put back where it belongs. This exercise is simple and very effective. When you can complete it, you'll discover that this experience no longer has any emotional hold on you. You'll be free of it, and free of all the ways in which it's been holding you back.

In this game, we take you to the cinema, to re-run your past experience from a very safe distance at the back of the theatre. Once you've finished this exercise, your fear is gone, never to return. This is because this game works the way your mind works; it changes your perspective and re-programs your mind, so that your fear no longer has any power over you.

Before you begin, decide what past experience you intend to heal.

Time Taken: 10 to 15 minutes

1. Sit comfortably and close your eyes

2. Imagine you are sitting at the very back of a large cinema. Way down at the front of the cinema is the screen. The lights are dimmed.

3. In a short while, a film will appear on the screen – a film of the first time you experienced your fear or trauma. If that makes you feel uncomfortable, move into the bullet-proof glass box up by the projection room and make yourself at home. This will keep you safe.

4. From this safe vantage point, breathe deeply and look down, down, through the vast empty theatre towards the screen. There on the screen is an experience from your past.

5. Know that you are safe, as you watch it from this distance. If it's too frightening for you, take refuge behind another layer of glass. Put the film into black and white and freeze the frame. Push it even farther away until you are comfortable watching this glimpse from your past. Once you're comfortable, run the film through to the end. It will probably only take a minute or so.

6. You may have some insights from that short film. If so, make a mental note of them.

7. Now that you have actually given your attention to this fearful experience, re-run the film, this time hitting the fast-forward button, so that the whole event is speeded up dramatically.

8. Repeat this; speed the film up even more until it's almost a blur on the screen, way down in front of you.

9. Now, run the film backwards. Watch as your response precedes the initial stimulus that frightened or upset you once upon a time.

10. Do another fast rewind on the film; repeat it until you begin to laugh at how silly it all looks, back to front.

11. At this point, that experience or trauma no longer has any hold on you. Open your eyes; take a few deep breaths. Really enjoy that feeling of release and relief that is sweeping through you. Your trauma is a thing of the past. (It always was).

15   Voice of the Critic

In this short exercise, you learn to silence your internal critic. Use it:

If ever you hear your internal critic telling you off for what you've done wrong
... or what you said or failed to say ...
... or if you've stepped out of turn

As women, we're particularly good at beating ourselves up. We all have the voice of the critic in our heads, and she can be brutal. She knows exactly what to say, and how to say it to make us feel we're no good and don't deserve better. And nothing saps your self-esteem quite like her scathing voice!

In this short exercise, we ask you to pay attention to your internal critic – for just long enough to render her remarks innocuous. So when you can give your full attention to this short exercise, and play full out, you'll simply brush off the remarks of your inner critic as if they were nothing – which of course they are. You'll no longer associate her sharp voice with self-criticism. Without her nagging and complaining, you'll begin to feel much better about yourself; you'll start to accept, love and respect yourself for the special woman you are.

Time Taken: 1 to 2 minutes

1. Find a place where you won't be disturbed.

2. Listen to your internal critic. What does her voice sound like? What's she saying to you right now?

3. Now, think of a man or male actor who really appeals to you – a man with a wonderfully sexy voice.

4. Repeat the same words of your critic, as he would say them, with his slow, sexy voice. Really get into it. This man wants to nibble your ear while he tells you *"how silly you are"* or *"how very stupid of you...."*

5. Whenever you hear the voice of your critic again, just call on that sexy guy to speak for her instead. If you need to, that is...

Repeat this exercise every day to feel really good about your body and yourself, and *actually change it* so it's more to your liking. Use it:

If you're dissatisfied and want to change the way you look
If you feel fat, ugly or unattractive
If you're tempted to judge other women on their attractiveness or the way they dress

As women, which of us hasn't at some stage wanted to change our bodies – to make ourselves more beautiful, more attractive, slimmer, trimmer, more curvaceous? The perception we have of our body is intimately caught up with the perception we have of ourselves – our relationship with ourselves.

There are two sides to this. Think about how you judge yourself. Consider how you judge other women who dress with more freedom – whatever they may look like. How do you respond to them? This gives you a good idea of how you feel about your own body, and how little or great you value yourself.

This exercise is one that helps you feel better about your body – and also helps you to shape it more to your liking. It is possible, within the constraints of your skeleton that is, to make lasting changes to how you look. It all begins in your mind.

So when you can repeat this activity every day for a month, you will see noticeable differences in your body – and in your relationship to it.

Before you begin, decide what you want. This is not a long list of what's wrong with you. Rather it's an image of how you want to look. Picture yourself with the body shape that really inspires you.

Time Taken: 2 to 5 minutes

1. Start to notice all your good features, all the things you like about yourself. Learn to appreciate your eyes, your skin, your nose, your chin.

2. See yourself in your mind's eye the way you want to look every day. Visualise yourself as if you already have the body you desire. You may want to stand in front of a mirror, or simply close your eyes. When you stop fighting your actual image, your unconscious mind will take on the new picture and help deliver it to you.

3. Find pictures of the body-shape you would like to have – one that is possible given your height and bone structure. This may be a picture from a magazine or a photo of how you looked at your best.

4. Put a few notes up around your mirror, on your wardrobe or dressing table to remind yourself of what you want. Just a single word, like *"slim"*, *"healthy"*, *"perfect skin"*. Your unconscious mind won't fight them. No affirmations, please. These only work if your unconscious mind believes in them, and what you want may be too much of a stretch. Copy those you want from the next page or make up your own.

5. Decide on one practical thing you can do today to take you a step closer to having the body you desire ... and do it.

6. You may want to do a few practical things to enhance your appearance. Get your hair cut in a new style that really suits your face, have a facial or a manicure. Find which colours suit you best with the services of a colour analyst or image consultant. Buy a new outfit that really suits your colouring, figure and personality.

7. Remember – your energy goes where you focus your attention. So you become what you think about and feel about all day long.

Be Beautiful

Attractive	Beautiful
Bright Eyes	Confident
Curvaceous	Desirable
Deliciously Desirable	Exquisitely Feminine
Fabulous	Fit
Friendly	Fun
Gorgeous	Healthy
In Control	Joyous
Looking Great	Lovely
Loving	Magnificent
Perfect Skin	Playful

Radiant	Radiantly Beautiful
Sensual	Sexy
Shapely	Slim
Stunning	Warm
Years Younger	

17   Chasing Clouds

This simple exercise can immediately lift your mood and make you feel great about yourself. Turn to it:

If you're feeling low or down
If ever you feel a negative emotion
If ever you want to feel good and get a real boost

Whilst it may seem strange to you, you can change your mood quickly, simply by changing your physiology – how you use your body. Mood is intimately tied to body posture; change your mood, your body posture changes. The opposite is also true – when you change your posture, you immediately change your mood. That's how this simple but powerful activity works.

When we feel down, our eyes are cast downwards; our shoulders are hunched over. Even our language tells us – *"I feel low; I feel down; I'm not looking forward to...."* When we feel great, our body is upright, our shoulders are back, our chest and heart area is open, our head is held high and our eyes are looking forwards and upwards. When you can remember to do this if you are feeling down, you'll immediately lift your mood, and be ready to take on the rest of your day.

Time Taken: Less than 1 minute

1. Whenever you feel any negative emotion, simply look up.

2. Count the cracks on the ceiling, count the roof-tiles on the building, see how many birds there are in the sky or watch the clouds pass by over-head.

3. Stretch your arms above your head, look up, smile and take a deep breath. It is impossible to feel depressed when you do this – your unconscious mind recognises this posture as one of happiness and well-being and immediately responds by sending happy hormones into your system.

4. Your posture will lift automatically and you'll feel really positive
    – and you'll find others around you copying you and catching
    your good mood.

Adding Spice

Enhance these good feelings with *37 Pump up the Volume* in the **indigo zone**.

Anchor this good feeling with *20 There's a Heroine* in the **yellow zone**.

This exercise gives you perspective on a situation that really troubles you – and diffuses its power. Use it:

If ever you "lose it"
If someone does or says something that upsets you
and you can't let it go
If you've had an argument
If you're angry or upset with someone

In situations like these, what we need is perspective. In this exercise we ask you to blast off – to get into an imaginary space craft and zoom off into space to a spot high above your problem. From that perspective, you get to look down on the situation, all the people involved in it including yourself, and see it for what it is.

When you can complete this exercise, you put distance between yourself and that experience. You see exactly what is going on with greater clarity, and learn the important lessons it is trying to teach you. Once you learn what you need to know, you emerge with the insights and resourcefulness you need to deal with it effectively. In future, you may well find that similar situations no longer push your buttons. You are free from getting stuck in that rut ever again.

Time Taken: 15 to 20 minutes

1. Sit quietly; you may find it helps to close your eyes.

2. Take a few moments to experience and acknowledge your problem, from where you are now. We're not asking you to re-run the event. Just pay attention to your thoughts and feelings. See what you see; hear what you hear; feel what you feel – right now, in this moment. Often we don't feel the feelings associated with the problem; we just stew about it in our heads.

4. Behind you your space craft is ready. Step into it and prepare to take off. Strap yourself in, as we begin the countdown. 10, 9, 8, 7, 6, 5, 4, 3, 2, 1 BLAST OFF!

5. As your rocket thrusts upwards, look down on that experience on the floor. It's getting farther and farther away – smaller and smaller – as you move steadily upward, until it's just a speck of dust on the surface of the earth.

6. From this perspective, look down on your problem. Keep your mind free. Pay attention to that speck of dust – your problem. What does it have to teach you? What can you learn from this experience?

7. Stay up there, looking down on your problem until you know you've learned all you need to learn from the experience. It may come to you in words, or pictures, or just as a feeling or insight. There may be no insights at all. Trust that this is exactly as it is meant to be.

8. Scoop up everything you've learned and put it into a large jar. Turn your space ship towards earth, and prepare for landing. You have a very magical ship that can land exactly where you took off from.

9. Once you touch down, come back into the room and back into your chair. Gently look again at your problem on the floor in front of you. Take the insights and learning you've received and pour them out of the jar into that situation.

10. When you're ready, open your eyes. It's sorted.

This is another exercise to give you perspective – this time from a point in the future – to resolve a problem or difficult situation. Turn to it:

> *If you've just had a bad experience that's left you pretty upset*
> *If you take to mulling it over in your mind*
> *If someone has done something to upset you*
> *If you've done or said something that you regret*
> *... and you can't let it go*

This fun game gives you a new strategy for dealing with problems. Traditionally, we women spend hours complaining and moaning, and not resolving our issues. This saps our energy and takes us away from living our lives fully.

Tip

One of the greatest problems we have is that we fail to *feel* our emotions. We talk about them; we push them away, we complain about them. But we seldom feel them. It is only when we feel our feelings fully that we can let them go. Otherwise they fester like an open wound, or get buried deep inside, causing illness.

You don't have to take your problems home. Use this exercise to deal with them in a fun and feminine way as they arise. That way you won't have the awful problem of having your man try to fix your problems. Men are action-orientated; they love to fix anything that's broken. Women are more sensual and feeling-orientated and we need to solve our problems in more heart-centred ways.

When you can remember to do this exercise next time a problem arises, you'll immediately feel better. You'll put that experience into perspective and easily let it go so that you can get on with the rest of your day.

Time Taken: 2 to 3 minutes

1. Find a place where you will not be disturbed, with enough space in front of you to walk at least 5 paces.

2. Look ahead of you, and imagine a path leading into your future.

3. You are standing at the start of that path, in your present, with this unpleasant experience. Take a moment to feel what it's like. See, hear, feel, taste and smell that experience fully.

4. Then take this bad experience off, the way you would a jacket, and drop it on the floor.

5. Walk forward into your future, leaving your bad experience behind. Take one, two, three or more paces, until you reach the point where this experience no longer has any power over you. How far into the future have you gone? You'll know instinctively. Just trust the answer you get.

6. Turn around from this future point, and look at your bad experience, lying in a heap on the floor at the start of your path. What have you learned from it? How do you feel about it now? What's it like for you right now? You may find yourself smiling or even laughing quietly to yourself...

Give yourself exactly the boost you need when you need it. Use this exercise:

> *Whenever you need a pick-me-up*
> *If your energy is waning*
> *When you need the confidence and self-assurance to speak up*
> *Whenever you want a feel-good fix*

There are times throughout the day when you just need a pick-me-up, a boost of energy, confidence or creativity. Here's a really easy way to give it to yourself. In fact, when you can understand and complete this activity, you'll always have exactly the resources you need when you need them most, to handle whatever life throws at you.

This activity is so effective because it locks in to the way your mind automatically works. It's a simple, yet powerful technique called a conditioned response or an anchor, because it anchors an emotionally charged experience with a particular stimulus. Once the association is made, that stimulus will automatically trigger the same response. This is a mental programme. It's how your mind works.

Your role in completing this activity is to create a positive, resourceful and emotionally charged state and anchor it to a simple stimulus. Your mind will do the rest.

Before you begin, choose your 'anchor'. This is the stimulus – usually a touch – that will automatically trigger your resourceful state whenever you need it. You may choose to touch your right ear lobe, or put two fingers on your left wrist. Find something that works really well for you.

Two things are important in selecting the anchor:

- *It needs to be an action that you can do anywhere without feeling conspicuous or embarrassed. In fact, it's best to choose an attractive habit you already have, such as gently touching your collar bone.*

- *It needs to be consistent – always touching yourself in the same place, with the same hand, same fingers, the same pressure and for the same length of time.*

Time Taken: 5 minutes to complete the exercise and set the anchor
Instantaneous to fire it

1. Find a place where you won't be disturbed.

2. Decide what resources will give you the best pick-me-up during the day. Three is a good number to begin with. You can add resources any time you wish.

3. You may choose confidence, courage, the ability to speak up for yourself, or see the other person's point of view. Only you know what is right for you right now.

4. Once you have decided on the resources you want at your disposal, bring each one up separately.

5. Remember a time when you had that resource – when you felt confident, or showed compassion, for example. Really experience what it is like for you. See what you see; hear what you hear; feel what you feel when you have that resource. Taste it, smell it if possible. Make the experience as real and as intense as you can.

6. When you have reached peak intensity with the experience, anchor it. Use the stimulus you have chosen and touch yourself there. Pay attention to the quality of that touch and its duration.

7. Take each additional resource in turn, and repeat steps 5 and 6.

8. Your resourceful state is now 'anchored'. You have a specific stimulus that you can trigger whenever you like, and it will

automatically bring back the same, highly-charged, positive and resourceful state you have just anchored.

9. You've trained your brain to deliver exactly what you want, when you want it.

10. Use it! Fire your anchor whenever you need those resources. Touch yourself exactly as you did when setting up the stimulus-response of this activity. Your mind will automatically deliver the goods. You'll immediately be in that resourceful state ready to handle whatever comes your way. It's magic!

11. Add further resources whenever you want or need them. Just identify the resource, and repeat steps 5 and 6.

Adding Spice

You will find a suggested list of resources in the Resources section of the Introduction. Use *37 Pump up the Volume* in the **indigo zone** to increase the intensity and power of your resources at steps 5 and 6. The more intense and emotionally charged the experience, the quicker and more easily the mind takes it on, and the more powerful the response to the same stimulus in future.

If you have a knee-jerk reaction you want to get rid of, this is the exercise for you. As you become more practiced, you will be able to complete this exercise in less than 5 minutes at your desk. Turn to it:

If you react badly to certain situations or people
and can't seem to change
If you have a knee-jerk reaction that you want to change
If you're running on automatic pilot and it isn't working for you

All of us suffer from knee-jerk reactions. It's the way our minds work. Some of these serve us very well: we don't have to re-learn to take our hand out of a fire if it is too hot. Once we learned these, we do them automatically. Some knee-jerk reactions are problematic, because they no longer serve us. They're inappropriate. Sometimes we find ourselves in the situation where we react to a certain person or situation by getting angry or frustrated. We fly off the handle, say things we never wanted to say, and end up feeling bad about it. If you're in this situation, you may not like your reaction. You may have tried and tried to change it without any success, and that only makes you feel worse – about it and about yourself. And whenever we feel bad about ourselves, we knock our self-esteem.

Remember, this is a program – an automatic response from your unconscious mind to a particular stimulus in the environment. It's one you learned early in life, and it no longer serves you. It keeps coming up again and again; trying to change it without using the power of your mind is futile, and probably why your earlier efforts haven't worked.

This exercise offers a simple, yet powerful way to eliminate this knee-jerk reaction from your life. When you can complete it, you cut the cord that binds you to that unwanted pattern of behaviour. Whenever a similar situation occurs in future, you are free to *choose* your response. Use it on as many old, unwanted patterns of behaviour as you like.

And it's no coincidence that we use your knees to make that change. We'll ask you to plant your knee-jerk reaction on one knee, and plant what you need to change that knee-jerk reaction on the other knee.

Then, nice and easy, you transfer what you need to the old pattern that no longer serves you, and the old pattern is destroyed.

You may find it easier to ask someone to talk you through it.

Before you begin, decide what behaviour pattern you want to change. Check out the Resources section in the Introduction.

Time Taken: 15 minutes first time through; 5 minutes thereafter

1. Find a place where you will not be disturbed. Sit down and make yourself comfortable.

2. Imagine you are in the situation that gives rise to this pattern and experience fully your reaction in as much sensory and emotional detail as possible.

3. At the peak of that experience, press your fingers firmly on your left knee. This anchors it there.

4. Give yourself a bit of a shake down. This helps to clear away the old pattern.

5. What do you need to change this pattern? Listen to your intuition. Let it guide you and take what words and ideas come to mind. If you have difficulty here, see the Resources section of the Introduction. Find at least three that will help you.

6. For each resource you have identified, think of a time when you had it, and begin to experience it fully. Bring all the sights, sounds and feelings of that resourceful state into your experience.

7. When you feel it really intensely, press your fingers firmly on your right knee. This is the opposite knee to where you anchored your unwanted reaction. Each time you anchor a resourceful state, use the same hand, the same fingers and the same pressure each time.

8. Repeat steps 6 and 7 for each resource you have identified.

9. When you have transferred what you need to your right knee, you are ready to make the change. You do this by taking everything you planted on your right knee and transferring them to the left knee – into the situation that needs them.

10. Place your fingers on your right knee, and say out loud – or to yourself.

   "I can take all I need to heal this situation from here (right knee) to where they are needed (left knee)."

11. Move your fingers from right knee to left knee. As you do so, you are transferring into the old pattern everything you need to behave differently. Keep doing this until you feel fine about it. The situation is healed.

Adding Spice

For more information on finding what you need to heal this situation, have a look at suggested resources in the Resources section of the Introduction.

Chapter 4

The Heart of the Matter

Chapter 4 The Heart of the Matter

Are you juggling too much?
Do you never have enough time?
Are you overstretched and out of sorts?
Do you find it hard to balance your work and home life?
Do you resent not taking time for you and you alone?

If so, you're in the **green zone,** needing to refresh your soul and restore balance and harmony to your life, to heal your inner and outer worlds.

Balance for many women now means drawing back into our feminine, the loving energy we have lost in our quest to be equals in a man's world of work. When we're out of our feminine – and many of us are – we lose connection with our natural innate power and extraordinary intuition. When we fail to honour who we are as women, our self-esteem can hit rock-bottom. It is in the **green zone** that we encourage you to *recover your feminine energy, to nurture and love yourself, to connect to your deeper self and to others in the workplace and at home.*

Green is the colour of hope, balance and harmony. Green is also the colour of the heart which is often depicted as having a pink centre. In the **green zone** you'll find exercises and tools to restore your balance and create harmony both within your body and spirit and in your environment. You'll discover how to heal and nurture yourself and how to give and receive in equal abundance.

When we ask women what they want most in life, they say they want joy, a deep fulfilling relationship, less stress and more personal time; but above all to be their authentic self. Now that you have completed the red, orange and yellow zones, you've cleared out many old unhelpful habits and beliefs that were holding you in their thrall, and re-built your self-esteem. You are now in a position to develop the joy and fulfilment that comes when you love and honour your true self, and practice being a more esteemed woman – both in your own eyes and in the eyes of those around you. For as you accept, love and respect yourself, you show others how to treat you – with the same respect and acceptance that you show yourself.

We women are acutely sensitive to our environment. It's the way we are made: to be aware at an intuitive level of both our physical and our emotional environments, and to monitor them carefully. When there is conflict or confusion, we become anxious and distressed; and the source of that anxiety may simply be an untidy desk, a chance remark or tripping over a pair of muddy football boots in the hall. And simple things like these can and do throw us off balance.

When you're overstretched and don't have time to think, and your boss, your kids, or your partner makes an unexpected demand on your time, it's enough to push you over the edge. You get angry; they get angry, and soon the whole situation has escalated out of control. It can be a vicious circle. Yet, when you can follow the instructions and do the exercises in this chapter, you'll have everything you need to break that vicious circle, to heal your heart and restore greater harmony and balance to your life.

1. You'll discover how making simple changes in your physical environment will calm your mind, lighten your mood, and improve your inner well-being.

2. You'll delight in awakening your senses to the magical world around you. Once you connect to this beauty, it will replenish and refresh you like never before. And that exquisite feeling of centeredness and oneness need never leave you.

3. You'll clear up unhealthy relationships and misunderstandings easily and quickly. You'll learn how to set boundaries and maintain them. As you set and respect your boundaries, others will recognize and respect them within you and within themselves as well. There is no greater gift you can give yourself – or them.

4. You'll discover how to take time for you and you alone, and how that very action actually frees up your time. You need never feel overstretched or be a slave to the clock again.

5. You'll learn to receive as well as give, and feel really good about it. You'll come to appreciate the goodness you already have, and be really grateful for it. This will recharge your flat batteries and restore balance in your life.

A woman who is not praised internally will wither, but as we are often our own worst enemies and our own worst critics, the most powerful form of praise comes from other women and from ourselves. When you can praise yourself first, you will be amazed how other people start to praise you too.

Practice this on a daily basis:

If you tend to criticize yourself a lot
If you hide your light under a bushel
If you wish someone would acknowledge who you are and what you have done
If you are longing for a pat on the back
If you live on your own

Tip

Susie did this with a small mirror for a few years and it was life-transforming. A few months ago she did this exercise with a full-length mirror – tears poured down her cheeks as she realised how much we condemn our beautiful selves and our precious life so often. It seemed as if she had only been affirming what she had done, rather than who she intrinsically was, so again she felt a big shift in her life.

We see our face in the mirror every day, and the tendency is to be critical in some shape or form. We find the one thing we hate most and focus on it, not realising that where our focus goes, our energy grows. We criticize our body, our face, our breasts, our hair, our freckles, our stupidity, our clumsiness, and we feed all those bad feelings even more. But it's about **who** you are, not just the packaging. When you start to become friendly with who you really are, your eyes start to shine, your self-esteem rises and you automatically take better care of yourself.

The eyes truly are the window of the soul and when you can look deeply into your own eyes and feel your own love and compassion and appreciation, untold wonders will occur.

Keep practising. This is vital work for us girls because when we are good to ourselves it nourishes something very deep inside. Don't think that you're going to get big-headed – this is never about vanity; it is about releasing pent-up sadness and healing a part of us which has not been sufficiently acknowledged.

Time Taken: 1 to 2 minutes as often as you like

1. Every time you do something well, or do something you were scared about doing – clearing your clutter, writing a work proposal, making a difficult phone call, going for an interview, winning an award at work, doing something new and challenging, getting out of a difficult situation, look in the mirror and say *"Well done. I'm really proud of you!"*

2. Look into your own eyes and find inspiring, motivating things to say. Tell yourself you're beautiful. Tell yourself you're amazing. Tell yourself you're special. Say *"Hello gorgeous,"* every time you pass a mirror; and soon you will start to mean it.

3. Find other wonderful things to say about you. Look at different parts of your body and admire them out loud. *"I love your breasts, I love your eyes, I love the way your eyes crinkle when you smile. I love your stretch marks that show you've given life. I love your thighs."*

4. Find other wonderful life-affirming things to say to yourself, about your achievements, your body, the love you give, your dreams and desires.

This exercise will make you realise how many years you've spent beating yourself up. This exercise enhances your worth. Soft encouraging words where we gently care for ourselves make such a difference. It all begins with loving and honouring ourselves.

Do it daily for three weeks for starters. Don't underestimate this – it's very powerful.

A great exercise to rest and refresh you. Turn to it:

If you're tired
If you're exhausted
If you're low on energy
If your nerves are putting you on edge
If you have lost focus
If you find it hard to concentrate

Let's face it: we get tired, mentally, physically, emotionally, spiritually. Susie and Almira were exhausted during the last phases of preparing this book. Like so many of you, we were pushing ourselves far too hard to meet a deadline, and as usual with women, striving for perfection. We consider ourselves fitter and healthier than most women our age, but our bodies let us know in no uncertain terms that it was time to rest. Susie developed an ulcer, and Almira sprained a muscle in her back. Why? We forgot to take some of our own medicine and do this exercise regularly.

You can't compare yourself to others. There will always be those who seem to have more energy than you do. We all have different pressures, have our own cares, worries and concerns to contend with, and respond to those stresses in our own way. When you do feel overwhelmed, or just plain tired, your body is telling you to rest. Yet we women are often the last ones to give ourselves that break. We push on regardless and put ourselves last, after the boss, our husband or partner, our children. If there's any time left over, we'll probably feel guilty taking it for ourselves.

And that means we shut off the part of ourselves that is creative and centred. To be true to our authentic selves, we must trust ourselves.

When you can do this exercise once a day, you'll give yourself permission to take time out for you and you alone, to rest and restore the

Tip
At work, women tend to breathe shallowly – like men. Yet, this is not how we are meant to breathe. Our breathing should come through the heart, because we are heart-centred beings.

delicate balance within. You'll refresh and recharge your batteries and return to your work with renewed energy, clarity and focus, and have much more to contribute. You'll discover that when you recognize that you are worthy of being loved, when you love and nurture yourself, your self-esteem will continue to grow.

Before you begin, *give yourself permission to rest*. This is important. If you go into this worrying about what others might think, or whether you should take the time off, you haven't really built sufficient self-esteem.

Time Taken: 10 to 15 minutes

1. Find a quiet place where you will not be disturbed and switch off your phone.

2. Lie down if you can, although it is not necessary. Otherwise sit comfortably. Close your eyes and allow your body to sink into the chair or into the bed.

3. Gently shut your eyes and keep your mouth half open as you pay attention to your breath. Sigh out any stress or tension; make a moaning noise as you begin to let go.

4. Now gently breathe in through your mouth or through your nose, and out through your mouth, lengthening each breath as you let go more and more.

5. Now imagine your breath entering and releasing through your heart.

6. As thoughts come into your mind, just gently drop them, and return to your breathing. (You may choose to repeat the sound *aahh*, or *oohh*, or *omm* on your out-breath to quiet your thoughts). Continue like this for 10 to 15 minutes.

7. You may find that insights come to you in this quiet time. They're one of the bonuses of giving yourself the rest you need.

This is a fun game to play to give and receive thoughtfully, without spending any money. Use it:

When you really want to treat someone you know
When you want to feel good by helping someone else
When you want to boost your self-esteem by giving that gift to another

Have you ever received a gift from someone and felt upset, angry or disappointed? Ten years after Almira had given up drinking coffee, her sister-in-law gave her an espresso coffee maker for Christmas. Susie had a similar experience. While she was running a thriving horticultural business, buying and selling plants all day long, her mother gave her a potted geranium for her birthday! How could they get it so wrong? We both felt awkward and deeply hurt, wanting to let them know they'd lost the plot completely, yet not wanting to offend. Like most of us, we decided to keep the peace and not say anything.

When it comes to giving, are we any better ourselves? How often do you stop to think what your loved ones really want? Do you give them what you think they'd like to receive, or what you'd love to receive instead? We heard a story of a man whose wife was ill in bed. He was deeply in love with her, and troubled by her illness. When he asked her what he could do for her, she asked him to bring her a bowl of a well-known brand of Cream

> **Tip**
> Giving has amazing qualities. When you give a thoughtful and heart-felt gift, you connect with that person; both of you receive immense joy and pleasure in the giving and receiving. And the more you give, the more you receive. Open your heart to both giving and receiving, and love and abundance beyond your wildest dreams will begin to flow into your life. You'll feel good about yourself; good about your loved ones. And you'll come to understand and appreciate them for who they are. Giving them permission to be who they are is the greatest gift you can give them.

of Chicken Soup. He found a can in the cupboard, but put it back, thinking his dear wife deserved much better. So he went out and bought some fresh chicken and vegetables, and spent the afternoon making her this wonderful, delicious soup with all the love he could muster.

When he brought it to her, she was so disappointed. What she wanted was exactly what she'd asked for – a bowl of canned soup – comfort food from her childhood.

When you can complete this exercise, you'll discover how to find a gift that would bring a huge smile of delight to a loved one's face. And in turn that will bring joy to your heart.

Time Taken A few minutes a day

1. Take some time to get to know your loved one and his or her interests and concerns. What's missing in their lives right now? What lights them up? What would really bring a smile to their face? What would really surprise and delight them? This is a gift that really acknowledges them, gives them immense pleasure.

2. Buy the gift in your mind. (You may hate it; you may think it's crass, or junk. But that's not the point. You're buying for someone else, and that someone will be delighted to receive it – especially if it comes from you!)

3. In your imagination, wrap it up. Find the right paper in your mind – paper they would find humorous or fun, romantic or beautiful – a paper which will touch them at their deepest.

4. Now in your imagination choose exactly the right card to go along with it. Is there a scent, or a place they love? Let the card remind them of those special times or places.

5. Give the gift in your mind. See the expression of joy and surprise on their face. Savour that moment of pleasure you both share.

6. Be grateful for having this special person in your life. If you like, make it part of your *Because*.

Adding Spice

29 *Because* in the **green zone**.

25   Clear that Clutter!

This simple exercise frees you up and restores your focus. Use it:

If you lose focus and find it hard to concentrate
If your mind is cluttered with too many thoughts
If you get discouraged because you never finish your "to-do" list

When you can follow this simple exercise through to the end, you discover a secret so profound you'll dance for joy. You see, as you change your physical environment for the better, you change your inner self for the better.

As you clear the clutter from your desk, you clear the clutter in your mind. As you throw the junk out of your home, all of a sudden, you find you have space to breathe, space to live and love, space for the magic to flow into your life. You free up your time and energy.

So many of us tend to accumulate stuff and it can quickly get to the point where we don't know what to do with it or where to put it in our over-crowded lives. It's always there, in the way. We pick it up dozens of times during the day when we don't need it, and can't find it when we do. It's frustrating, and a waste of time and energy.

Tip

Most of us overestimate what we can do in a day, and underestimate what we can do in a year, and this leaves us feeling inadequate on a daily basis, and unfulfilled over the year. When you make a list of what you want to accomplish the night before, you arrive at work the next day with a clear mind – never mind the state of the desk. Whilst it's so much easier to work from a clear desk, it's actually easier to come to work with a tidy mind and an untidy desk than the other way around. As you focus on what matters, you begin to fulfil yourself, and nurture your self-esteem. And there's no loss of creativity here. Both Susie and Almira used to think that pre-planning meant they were in a straight-jacket for the day, until they discovered that forward planning gives you focus and instead of stifling creativity, gives you the process and discipline to be more creative.

STOP right NOW! Clear that clutter!

The very thought of doing so may fill you with dread. It always seems to take so long to go through all the stuff cluttering your desk, filling up the back room, or lurking in the garage. So often, we spend most of our time wondering what to do with things, and it takes up space in our mind – rent free!

Here's the quick way to get it done

Before you begin, find a large sturdy box, and put a label on the top of it with today's date on it.

Time Taken: Allow yourself 15 minutes to clear your desk; up to an hour to clear some space in the garage.

1. Pick up the first thing in the area you plan to clear, and ask yourself:
    "Do I need this?"
    "Do I love this?"

2. If the answer to either question is yes, put it away where you can find it easily.

3. If the answer to both questions is "no", and you haven't the heart to let it go, put it in the box. Otherwise throw it out or give it away.

4. Continue in this vein until you have cleared the area.

5. Store the box away, making sure the date is on the label. Keep it for six months. Your "stuff" is there should you need it.

6. If you haven't pulled anything out of the box in that six months, get rid of its contents – sell it on e-bay, give it to charity, or throw it out.

This is a delightful activity to feed body and soul. Turn to it:

When you need to restore your balance
When you need some quiet time for you
Whenever you feel you need to recharge your batteries

Find a park, square or garden close to your workplace, or en route, and do this for a few minutes on your way into work, or over lunch. Take as much time as you like. 30 minutes to 1 hour is really good for body and soul. However, even 5 minutes will make a huge difference to your well-being.

When you can allow yourself to become fully immersed in this, you are filled to overflowing with joy, and a deep love for all that is. You delight in each and every one of your senses. You discover the beauty and magic of this precious world. You know without doubt that everything and everyone within it is working in your favour, because you are connected with a greater power that runs in and through you – that *is* you. And you emerge from it relaxed, replenished and refreshed.

Before you begin, select your paradise. Go to a park, some woodland, or set out along a beach or river bank. Find a spot in nature that speaks to your soul. You can find these, even in crowded cities.

Time Taken: 5 minutes or longer

1. Set out for a leisurely stroll.

2. Open your eyes to the world around you. Notice the colours of the sky, the foliage, the earth, the water, the play of light and shadow. Watch the shimmer of the sun across the water, the dancing reflections. See the shafts of silvery gold light streak through the branches of the trees, or the bright sunflowers tilt their heads towards the light. Really **see** what is.

3. Now open your ears to the sounds of the world around you. Can you hear the birds sing? The rustle of the leaves, the trickle of a

brook or the crashing of the waves. Do you hear dogs barking, or the distant sound of traffic? Really **hear** what is.

4. Now open your sense of touch to the world around you. Feel the delicate frond of a leaf, the rough texture of a tree trunk, the warmth or the chill in the air, the cold wetness of the water. Feel the sun warm your back, the gentle breeze caress your face. Really **feel** what is.

5. Now open your nose to the world around you. Breathe in the damp leaf mould, the scent of wild honeysuckle, or the fragrance of geraniums. Smell the dust in the air, the fresh scent of pines after the rain. Really **smell** what is.

6. Now open your mouth to the world around you. If you can, really **taste** what is.

7. Continue like this for as long as you like, really seeing, hearing, feeling, tasting and smelling the world around you.

8. Before long, your mind goes quiet and you discover the magic of being fully present, just you and the world of your senses. You find you are back in touch with who you really are, feeling fully alive, your body refreshed and your balance restored. There is no greater boost to your self-esteem than this.

This is a fun activity to help you set and keep boundaries so that you can care for and nurture yourself. Use it:

If you feel someone is walking all over you
If ever you feel vulnerable
If you find it hard to know where your boundaries are
If you're inclined to apologise for your very existence
If ever someone oversteps the mark and invades your space

Tip

I'm sure you've all had the experience – the very uncomfortable experience – of being in a crowded room or train, crammed up against a lot of strangers who are invading your space. We have an innate sense of the physical space around our bodies. When strangers invade this space, we feel violated. The same is true of emotional intrusions. That's why knowing and having the strength to maintain our physical and emotional boundaries is essential to our self-esteem and our well-being.

Each of us needs to set and keep boundaries. It's one of the most important ways in which we care for and nurture ourselves, in which we honour and respect who we are. It is also one of the most important ways in which we honour and respect those around us – in our work and home environments.

Yet, as women, we either set up prickly forests around ourselves, or find it difficult to set boundaries, and even more difficult to maintain them. It's so natural for us to give, to nurture and support others, often at the expense of our own well-being. We may feel tired, guilty or resentful when helping others, and those feelings only serve to poison our relationships so that no one benefits. We're acting out of duty, not love. We allow others to violate our boundaries because we don't know where they are or how to keep them intact. And that really damages our self-esteem.

When you can complete this exercise, you soon discover the important distinction between giving *of* yourself and giving *up* yourself. You learn how to give *of* yourself, so that everyone benefits. You learn to know what is acceptable to you in every situation, at work and at home. And as you respect your boundaries, those around you will come to acknowledge and respect them in you. And you soon recognize and respect the boundaries in others as well. This is a healthy way to continue to feed your growing self-esteem.

Time Taken: Less than 5 minutes

1. Imagine you have a beautiful golden egg. Step into it whenever you wish. When inside you can stretch up and just touch the ceiling, and when you stretch your arms out in all directions, you can just touch the sides. There is room inside for you to do and be all you are meant to be.

2. Your golden egg is permeable to air, to love and to light. All these nurturing elements and every other good thing can pass through to you and out from you. Yet the egg protects you from the outside world. It gives you your boundaries.

3. In stressful situations, expand your golden egg to increase your boundaries and give you more space to breathe freely.

4. In loving situations, you can dissolve it to enjoy the intimacy that nourishes you and your loved ones.

5. Whenever you are inside your golden egg, you are protected. There is a glow about you because you know you are safe. And you give off a different energy, an energy that encourages others to respect your boundaries and their own.

This is a great exercise to make your day special. Use it:

> *If ever you feel a bad hair day coming on*
> *When you want to make today special*
> *Whenever you feel like giving someone a treat*

When you can remember to do this exercise every day, you can't help but have another great day – feeling good all day long.

Before you begin, set your intention to have a great day. Set the intention when you go to bed and again when you wake up. There is no particular process to this, just select whatever activities appeal to you, or find your own.

Time Taken: A minute or two, throughout the day

1. Play your favourite music. Hum the tune. Singing allows your spirit to soar (even if you're tone deaf and can't sing for love or money, give it a go in the privacy of the bathroom.)

2. If possible, dance to your favourite music. Just let yourself go.

3. Perform a random, anonymous act of kindness.

    - Let someone into the queue ahead of you.

    - Greet everyone on your way into work with a cheerful "*Good Morning*". You'll be surprised at the responses you get.

    - Let the first thing you say to someone be something to brighten their day.

    - Place a cut rose on the desk of a co-worker you find irksome, and just observe their reaction

    - Make a pact with the waiter, and treat the strangers at the next table to their morning coffee without their knowing anything about it.

4. Keep random acts of kindness anonymous. They give most pleasure when the recipient doesn't know where it comes from.

5. Notice how good it makes you feel to give, without asking anything in return.

6. Before long, you'll be surprised with the many random acts of kindness that come your way.

7. Enjoy them. Appreciate them. Know your life is rich and abundant beyond measure.

This joyful exercise makes you aware of how rich and abundant your life is. Use it:

If you feel as if the world is against you
If you think you're not getting what you want or deserve
When you need to take time out for you
Whenever you really want to nurture yourself
Every day, to feel great about yourself

There is always something to be thankful for in our lives, whether we are aware of it or not. Gratitude is a great catalyst in increasing our joy and happiness, in stepping us up the ladder to more and more positive energies and emotions. You see, the more grateful you are, the better you feel and the more things you have in your life to be thankful for.

Whatever your situation, when you can complete this exercise you begin to appreciate how rich and rewarding your life is. The more frequently you do this activity, the more you notice and appreciate the good things you already have to be grateful for. And the more you attract positive experiences into your life.

Before you begin, you will need a notebook or a piece of paper and a pen.

Time Taken: Up to 30 minutes

1. Think of something you love to do, or someone you love.

2. Take a page and list all the reasons why you love that person or enjoy doing that thing. **Because** he or she ...

3. When you're done, write down answers to these questions:

    "What is it that makes them special to you?"

    "How do you feel about them?"

4. Keep writing until you're done.

5. Repeat this activity whenever you like. Or review the pages you've written to remind yourself of whom and what you love, and why.

Chapter 5

Thinking Makes It So

Chapter 5 Thinking Makes It So

Do you sometimes find it hard to think clearly?
Do you try and try and still find it hard to get what you want?
Are your thoughts getting you down?
Do you procrastinate?
Does your head pull you one way and your heart another?
Do you agonize over decisions, and often regret the choices you made?
Are you terrified of public speaking?

If so, you're in the **blue zone**, finding it hard to think clearly because your head is stuffed full of thoughts, needing to make important decisions and being all too aware of the struggle between your mind and your emotions in the choices you make.

> *Tip*
> Remember, you can always change a thought, and in doing so, you can transform your life situation overnight.

Blue is the colour of choice and self-expression. In the **blue zone**, you will discover games, exercises and activities to voice your thoughts and express yourself freely. You'll learn to make decisions you won't later regret.

Blue is the power of our words, our thoughts and our language in creating our reality. The **blue zone** will increase your awareness of your thoughts, and how the language you use affects your emotions and your reality. You'll discover how to *create a better life for yourself, by using your thoughts in more positive and focused ways.*

You may not realise it, but every thought you have, every word you utter and every choice you make has far-reaching consequences, not just for you but many people around you, even people you don't know. The quality of your questions determines the quality of your answers; the quality of your answers determines the quality of your life. When you learn to ask better questions, you get better answers, and that leads to greater clarity in your thinking and more direction and purpose in your life.

Thoughts are a form of energy, and energy sticks to you. High energy thoughts are powerful programs, patterns of behaviour that are quickly and easily installed in our minds. Once there, we automatically act out the program, without thinking about it. This is how our minds work. And the thoughts we feed our mind determine the quality of our lives.

You now know that many of the incessant, repetitive thoughts in your head don't belong to you. They are the words – often installed as powerful programs – of your parents, teachers and other influential people in your life. In earlier chapters, we introduced exercises and activities to clear out these old programs that no longer work for us, often replacing them with more appropriate behaviour. Now it's time to move on to the next stage, where you take charge of your thoughts and use them to create the life and lifestyle you want for yourself.

When you can complete the exercises in this chapter, you discover how to make decisions that are right for you, easily and effortlessly, knowing full well the implications your choices have for you and those around you. In doing so, you connect to and strengthen your personal authority, and your self-esteem increases by leaps and bounds.

1. You learn to express yourself freely and fully using voice and movement and discover that when you have self-esteem, you aren't concerned about what others think of you. Once you've experienced this freedom, there is no stopping you.

2. You discover the power of your words – how language affects who you are and how you feel, and how to use your words and your thoughts – to give yourself more of what you want to experience in your life. When you invite what you want into your life, what you want begins to appear as if by magic. The more you practice this, the more effective you become in consciously creating the life you want – the life and lifestyle you know you deserve.

This is a terrific game to make you feel *"top of the pile"*. Use it often:

> *If you're self-conscious in front of others*
> *If you feel awkward in company*
> *If you need to speak in public*
> *If you're too concerned about what others think to be yourself*
> *When you really want to feel like a star*

Every time you do this, you learn to express yourself more fully through dance and movement. Don't be fooled. Whilst this game looks simple, it is profound because it works at several levels at once – physically, emotionally, psychologically. The more you let yourself go and get fully into the spirit of the game, the more fully expressed, the more confident and self-assured you will become.

We need to regain our sense of flow in our movement which has been stifled by working in intense masculine environments. When you can play this full out, your attitude to yourself and to life will improve dramatically. You'll drop any concerns you have about what others think of you; your self-consciousness will disappear, and you'll enjoy being who you are in any company.

Before you begin, you'll need a copy of Frank Sinatra singing "New York, New York". Put it on and turn up the volume good and loud.

Time Taken: 3 minutes

1. While the music plays, you're the star. You're on a red carpet outside the cinema for the first night of your performance. The crowds are gathered five deep along the carpet to the stage door – just to see you. They're cheering you on, whistling, clapping, reaching out to touch your hand. They love you!

2. Listen to the music, and begin to dance down the carpet. Swing around, blow kisses to the crowd, throw open your arms! Act and dance as if you really are *"A number 1, top of the heap"*

3. Greet your fans. Move gracefully, move with confidence, knowing that you're the star!

4. Play it again. Before long, you'll be hearing *"New York, New York!"* in your head whenever you enter a room, walk down the corridor, get out of a taxi or step off a plane. And, wherever you are, you'll find yourself moving in time to the music, with the same easy confidence and adulation.

5. Enjoy this game. Play it fully. Play it all out!

This little girl game really makes you aware of your words. Turn to it:

If your thoughts are getting the better of you
If you feel you're not getting what you deserve at work or at home
If you're sceptical
If you don't believe that thinking makes it so

"Sticks and stones may break my bones, but words will never hurt me!"

Tip

If you're like the rest of us, you have endless thoughts running through your mind all the time – welcome thoughts, unwelcome thoughts, repetitive thoughts, self-deprecating thoughts or plans for your future...

What you may not appreciate is that your mind is programmed by your thoughts. The unconscious mind in particular simply does what we ask it to do, no questions asked. So, the more you think a particular thought – whatever it happens to be – the more likely it is to become ingrained in your unconscious mind. The more intensely you experience that thought, the more effective the programming becomes.

The greatest challenge is in becoming aware of your thoughts – and what impact they are *really* having on your life situation. For example, whenever you say *"yeah, but"*, you make your butt bigger, because you're saying *"yes"* to your butt!

Did you kid yourself whenever you used this expression as a child? Almira certainly did, valiantly claiming that words could never hurt her, despite the fact that some bully boy had just wounded her with his brutal, cutting remarks.

Words can hurt; they can also heal. Words can destroy; they can also create anew. Words can elate us; they can take the wind from our sails. Words are incredibly powerful in making or breaking our self-esteem. And yet for the most part, we pay very little attention to them. We all have our favourite expressions – the ones we come out with time and again. We are constantly bombarded by the words of others. When Almira held a high powered management role in the IT industry, her male colleagues referred to her as a hard-nosed bitch, a compliment in their eyes and a real insult in hers!

What do our words really say about us? How do the words of others affect us? What effect do these words have on you, on your emotions, or how you value yourself? When you can play this game even a few times, you'll discover just how the words you use and the words you hear every day affect your feelings and transform your mood for good or bad. And with that new awareness, you'll begin to choose your words more carefully, selecting those which make you feel good and bring joy and fulfilment into your life, and avoiding those that make you feel bad.

Before you begin, you will need some coloured crayons or coloured pens and some paper.

Time Taken: 2 to 5 minutes

1. Make a list of words and expressions you use all the time. You can also use the list included overleaf. Print them on a sheet of paper, cut each word or expression out separately, fold each one up and put them in a basket, an envelope or a bowl. Keep this and use it each time you play the game.

2. Pick a word out of the bowl and write it down on the top of a sheet of paper; then put the original word back in the bowl.

3. Close your eyes and really feel the word or expression and what it means to you.

4. Then take your crayons or coloured pens and draw what the word or expression makes you feel, what it makes you see or hear. Forget trying to be an artist. You are doing this for you, no one else, and it doesn't matter what this looks like. It could be a lot of black zigzags or red splotches if that's what the word does for you. Or it could be expansive clouds and magenta sunsets. These are your feelings. They're just for you.

5. Take a moment to look at your word picture. How does it make you feel? What insights do you get about this word?

6. When you play this repeatedly, you may find that certain words and expressions keep cropping up for you. Your unconscious mind is drawing them to your attention. If so, please give them extra attention.

7. Use the powerful insights of this exercise to put more of the good words into your vocabulary and stamp out the more negative ones.

Energy Words

Angry	Bitch
Black	Bliss
Childlike	Exhausted
Freedom	Frustrated
Glory	Happiness
Helpless	Hopeless
Joy	Love
Prostitute	Red
Relax	Stress
Stupid	Time out
Tragedy	Victim

| Wiped out | Whore |

| Wonder | Work |

This is a great exercise to improve your self-expression and with it your self-esteem. Turn to it:

If you find it hard to speak up for yourself
If you're embarrassed by the sound of your voice
If you need to speak in public and are terrified at the prospect
If you're often tongue-tied

We are really surprised when we hear recordings of our voice because that's not how we hear ourselves speak. The vibration of our voice goes through various bony structures and fluids and gets distorted before we hear the end result. Interestingly when people listen to us, they take more notice of the sound and tonality of our voice together with our posture and physiology, than they do of the actual words we use.

When you can learn to enjoy your voice, you will feel much more comfortable speaking in public. These exercises are great fun, and you can do them anywhere you choose – when you're doing the washing up, when you're driving or in the bathroom where you get instant feedback. Your lips, tongue and mouth become like an echo chamber and you can change the sound and projection in many different ways. You don't have to sound like an opera singer, or like your favourite rock band – just enjoy playing with sound, and always with a smile on your face.

Time Taken: 5 minutes

1. Sing the letter a – you can do it as "*ay*" and as "*aaah*". Sing up and down the scale, loud and soft, opening your mouth widely, then with your lips almost closed. What feels and sounds best for you?

2. Sing the letter e – "*eeee*" and notice how the sound differs when you smile.

3. Sing the letter i – sounding like "*eye*" – again try opening your mouth really wide, then half closed.

4. Sing the letter o – try it as an *"oooh"*; try it with eyes closed, eyes open, as a whisper, as a shout, short and sharp or long and drawn out.

5. Sing the letter u – as in *"you"* – see how many different ways you can change the sound and volume by moving your lips and your jaw

6. Now sing *a – e – i – o – u* – over and over again, going up and down the scales.

7. Now practice singing your conversations – do it with friends in different styles – opera, pop, rap, ballad.

Use this before you make a decision and you won't regret it.

If you dread making decisions
If you're prone to procrastinate and put things off
If you often regret the decisions you make
When you want to understand what might happen if...

Decision comes from the Latin *decidere*, and it means to cut out any other possibility. When we think of it this way, making the right decision can be a challenge. Often, we go on what we feel is the right thing to do, without realising that what feels right is not necessarily the same as what feels good. It's in our nature to avoid confrontation in our work or home environment. To do so, we may find ourselves making compromises – decisions that just feel wrong. And making the wrong decision can often lead to feelings of low self-worth and self-esteem.

We have an innate knowing of what is good and true. As children we are taught to let our conscience guide us, but sometimes in the thrust of the business world we forget to tap into this resource. If there is a chance of hurting or damaging someone by our actions, we intrinsically know, as deep inside, it really does not make us feel good – maybe justified, maybe great on the surface, but deep down in our innermost being, not good. This is not a moral issue but a feeling that acts as our guidance system.

Perhaps you know someone who really fancies her boss, and it feels right to go to bed with him. At a superficial level she may feel great, but deep down inside she will not feel good. What are the consequences? Let's track them down. Say she decides to sleep with him; it becomes common knowledge in the office, and soon everyone is gossiping about it. Perhaps her colleagues snigger as she walks past, or assume that any praise or recommendation she gets is because of her intimacy with the boss, rather than on her merit. She loses credibility. His wife and her husband feel cheated. There might be any number of potential consequences here for both of them, their marriages and their children; the boss's boss finds out, disciplines her boss and has her fired.

Tracking it down is about understanding the consequences of your decisions *before* you make them. This forces you to respect yourself, to move forward from a position of grace where you know you are not hurting anyone, yourself included. When you take responsibility for your decisions and actions, your self-esteem is assured.

So, when you can follow this approach whenever you have an important decision to make, you make the good choice – one that makes sense; one that feels good – indeed, is good – for you right now. And you discover the magic that flows into your life once your mind is clear and focused and your heart in perfect alignment. You feel calm and clear about your choice, knowing nothing is niggling you. It's as if the voice inside your head is saying *"You're on track!"* We know you as women will understand this because we women have an innate sense of what is good and just.

You may find it useful to write this down. If so, have a pen and paper handy.

Time Taken: 15 minutes or so

1. For the choice or decision you have to make, ask yourself:

    "What options do I have?"
    "Which ones feel good for me?"

2. Take what feels good and ask yourself:

    "What would happen if I chose this option?"
    "What are the consequences of this for me?"
    "What are the consequences of this for those I work with?
    For those I love?"

3. Track the consequences down another stage or two so that you really understand what could happen if you took this decision, and how it affects you and others around you.

4. Once you're clear about the implications of your options, ask yourself:

"In choosing this option, in taking this course of action, am I meeting my real needs?
And the real needs of others who matter to me?"

5. If your answer is "YES", move on to step 6. If "NO", find another option and repeat from step 2.

6. Once you have an option that makes sense, ask yourself:

    "Am I being honest with myself?"
    "Does this feel good? Do I really trust my intuition?"

7. If you answer "NO" to any of these, go back to step 2 and find a better option.

8. If you answered "YES" to these questions, continue:

    "What would I decide if I weren't afraid?"
    "What would I do if I knew I deserved better?"

9. You may find new options you want to look at. If so, loop back through the process to make sure that what is good for your heart makes sense for you and others who matter to you.

10. Continue to loop through this process until you're really satisfied with your decision. It is one that feels good; one that makes sense; one that leaves you in no doubt whatsoever that you have made the right choice.

11. Go with your decision. If at a later stage, circumstances change in unforeseen ways and your decision no longer feels good and true, please re-evaluate it and change your mind if you need to.

This delightful exercise encourages you to do more of what you love. Use it:

Whenever you want to feel good
If you feel you're acting more out of duty than love
Every day to improve your happiness

As women, we feel we are there to help, to give of our time, of ourselves. And often, we fail to make that important distinction between giving *of* ourselves – which is natural – and giving *up* ourselves, which weakens us, damages our self-esteem and can spoil our relationships.

Much of the time we are being dutiful. Rather than doing what we love with the people we love, we often spend our time doing what others want and expect of us. This may be in conflict with our personal value system and so it wears us out, frays our nerves, and – if we are really honest about it – can poison our relationships with the very people who matter most to us.

This exercise encourages you to think about what you love to do, and asks gently that you start to include those things you love into your daily routine. When you can complete this exercise, you discover what you really love and take time to do something that gives you pleasure every day. As you do more of what you love, more love and beauty flows into your life, and your relationships blossom, because you are there because you choose to be, and not from a sense of duty.

Time Taken: You will need 30-40 minutes to create your list in a single sitting.

1.   Take a pen and paper and begin to list all the things you love to do. Be really honest. This list is for YOU; you don't need to please anybody else, and you'll miss the spirit of the game if you do.

2. If you find it hard to get started, let your mind drift back to your childhood, or your teens. What did you love to do as a child? Write it down.

3. Keep adding to the sheet until you have at least 100 things that you love to do.

4. Each morning, take at least one of your 'favourite things' and do them that day. Savour the time you spend doing what you love. Enjoy it.

5. And appreciate it!

Adding Spice

Magnify the results of this exercise with another that really makes you appreciate all the good things in your life – 29 *Because* in the **green zone,** or include them in your *42 Gratitude Journal* in the **violet zone.**

35　Top 10

This exercise makes you feel great. Just do it.

Your Top 10 are the feelings that make you feel really great. Like the top 10 singles on the hit parade, you're at your best when you play these feelings over and over again throughout the day. Putting them on cards you can carry in your bag will remind you to play another great feeling and be on top of the world.

When you can remember to follow through on this exercise every day, you begin to create a very different world for yourself. You lift your mood and feel the way *you* want to feel, in any moment or situation throughout the day. You choose the way you respond to others; you create the life you want. As you brighten your mood and feel better about yourself, others recognize the change in you and treat you differently – with more pleasure and respect. All you need to do is take out a card and do what it says. Easy!

By way of preparation, list your top ten feelings. Remember to include those that really make you feel great – romantic love, happiness, joy, bliss, excitement, sensuality, compassion, freedom, peace, humour, gratitude, gracefulness – whatever you know feels good for you.

Time Taken: 1 minute. Thereafter, you can stay in your new feeling for as long as possible

1. Select from the Top 10 overleaf, or use blank cards to record the 10 feelings that are most meaningful to you. Keep the cards in an envelope or small box.

2. Every morning, take one card out of your Top 10 box at random and make a point of playing that hit feeling today.

3. Have a practice session before you leave the house. Really experience your Top 10 feeling fully.

4. Anchor the feeling for later. See *There's a Heroine*.

5. As many times as you can throughout the day, bring up this great feeling.

Adding Spice

20 There's a Heroine in the **yellow band** to anchor your great feeling.

Your Top 10

Accepting	Alive
At Peace	Blissful
Compassionate	Confident
Content	Courageous
Eager	Energetic
Enthusiastic	Free
Generous	Grateful
Happy	Joyful
Loved	Loving
Optimistic	Passionate
Peaceful	Positive

Quiet		Relaxed
Willing		

Chapter 6

Using Your Mind for a Change

Chapter 6 Using Your Mind for a Change

Do you set goals for yourself and never accomplish them?
Are you unhappy with your circumstances yet can't seem to change them?
Do you fail to appreciate how lucky you are?
Do you want to have more, do more, be more?
Do you feel you're ready to give something back?
…To make a contribution?

If so, you're in the **indigo zone**, ready and willing to discover and achieve what you really want, but without necessarily having the tools to do so easily.

You are now at the point where your self-esteem has increased dramatically and this new, more positive sense of self is well-established. There may be times when circumstances shake you a bit, times when you relapse, but they should now be few and far between. You have the tools in the earlier chapters of the book to deal with these if they arise.

From here on, we invite you to discover and learn to achieve what it is you truly want. At first, this may feel strange. You may never have taken the time to give yourself the gift of becoming more of who you truly are. Now is your opportunity to engage your imagination and open your mind to what is possible in your life; to explore a few simple, yet powerful ways in which you can focus and discipline your mind to begin to realise them. It is now time for you to grow the power of your mind to draw to you the people, experiences and other resources you need and want in order to achieve your dreams and goals. This is what the **indigo zone** is all about. It's about *reinforcing your self-esteem and making it part of who you are.*

Indigo is the colour of wisdom, truth and intuition. It reminds us that each of us has a unique contribution to make to the lives of others and the world. In the **indigo zone**, you'll discover how to develop the power of your mind to consciously create the life and lifestyle you desire.

You'll find tools to discover your purpose, to set goals so that you cannot fail to achieve them.

It takes practice to gain mastery over our thoughts and feelings. So often, they tend to drift back to our present circumstances, to what we're unhappy about in our lives. And when this happens, we stay there – until we consciously choose to make a change.

Now is your opportunity to break that pattern, and learn to create what you want for yourself. The first stage of this is noticing what is good in your life already, and enjoying and appreciating that to the full. Gratitude is a powerful magnet, drawing into your life more things to be grateful for. The second stage is to take time out to set your goals, focus your mind and discipline your imagination to deliberately create your future.

The exercises in the **indigo zone** take you through a process designed to develop mastery of your mind. Remember, it takes practice. The more you play with these exercises and enjoy the experience, the more skilled you will get at mastering your mind.

When you can complete the exercises in this chapter, you will know through direct experience the power of your mind to attract into your life anything you choose. You learn powerful techniques to set goals and create the future you want to enjoy. And use the extraordinary capability of your mind to instil those goals and dreams into your unconscious, so that it delivers them to you easily and seemingly effortlessly.

1. You learn how to set your goals and visualise your dreams in the juicy detail you need to store them in your unconscious mind. You discover tools and techniques to increase their impact so that the unconscious mind cannot help but accept them as real right now. (Your unconscious mind lives only in the present. It has no sense of past history or future aspirations, so when it takes on your goal as real it is real right now.)

2. You discover a simple, yet powerful technique to appreciate all the good things you currently have in your life, and tools to enhance any good feeling you have, so that you always feel blessed.

This is a great little exercise to make you appreciate just how good your life already is. Use it:

If ever you find yourself focusing on what's missing or wrong with your life
If you find fault with those around you
If you feel your life really isn't up to scratch
If you start complaining about how bad it all seems

When we look at our lives, we often focus on what's missing, what's wrong – or not right – with it. Seldom do we take the time to stop and appreciate what is really good with it. Yet, by doing this, we open ourselves up to the most exquisite experiences of joy and aliveness that immediately transform our view of ourselves and of what is possible for us to achieve now and in the future.

The more frequently you do this exercise, the better you feel and the more practiced you become in drawing feel-good feelings into your experience. Indeed, when you can practice this for a few minutes every day, you transform your life. You get into the habit of attracting to you all that you love, appreciate and enjoy. And knowing that you can do this empowers you. It further builds your self-esteem and leaves you confident in your ability to take charge of your own life. Make a habit of this every day.

Before you begin, have a pen and notebook to hand. You may want to write down your experiences to enhance the value and power of this activity.

Time Taken: Set aside 15 minutes a day to do this for the first week or so. Thereafter, it will come naturally.

1. There is really only one rule – appreciate! Appreciation is a catalyst – just the same way money appreciates in your savings account, the more you do this exercise, the more you get back. Appreciation is a secret ingredient that immediately improves

your emotional state, boosts your physical health and well-being.

2. Look around your immediate environment, and calmly and gently notice something that pleases you. Choose only objects that capture your attention and easily please you.

3. Hold your attention on this pleasing object. Consider how useful, wonderful or beautiful it is. The longer you focus on it the more your positive feelings will increase.

4. Notice your improved feelings and be grateful. Use *Pump Up the Volume* to make that feeling stronger and stronger.

5. When you write down your experience, you will find this exercise even more powerful and fast-acting.

6. Look around and find a second thing that pleases you and repeat the process.

7. Remember, appreciation is a catalyst! The more you use it, the more good feelings you attract into your life.

Adding Spice

37 Pump up the Volume on the next page will greatly enhance your positive feelings.

Here's a fun game to greatly enhance your great mood or feeling. Use it:

When you want to feel really great
When you feel great and want to feel even better
When you want that great feeling to last

When you're in a good mood, you are really aligned with who you are and what you are here to do. All too often, though, that great mood can quickly evaporate. There's really no need for this – there are ways of augmenting your wonderful mood. And there are ways of making feeling good a permanent fixture in your life.

It's simple. You turn up the volume of that great feeling, and at peak intensity, set a stimulus that you control using *There's a Heroine*. Every time you give yourself that stimulus, you experience your great feeling.

When you can remember to do this exercise whenever you're in a great mood, you dramatically improve it – yes, it is possible. Coupled with *There's a Heroine*, you have great feelings literally at your fingertips, any time you choose. And it's a great way to enjoy an orgasm on your own!

You can do this exercise for yourself, or ask someone to do it for you. If you choose the latter, make sure your friend is respectful of you and the process.

Before you begin, review *There's a Heroine* if you want to be able to access this great feeling anytime you choose. Or just enjoy this exercise on its own.

If you're not already in a good mood, get into one, by thinking of a time when you felt terrific. Bring that experience up fully; really feel what it's like to feel great. See all you see. Hear what you hear. Feel all you feel. Taste and smell whatever you do.

Time Taken: Less than 5 minutes

1. Find a place where you won't be disturbed.

2. When you're in a really good state, pretend your left arm is the volume control of a stereo. Take your right finger and place it on your left wrist and slowly move it up your arm to increase the volume, i.e. the intensity of the experience.

3. As you do so, remind yourself that you are increasing the volume, increasing the intensity of your feelings. They get more and more powerful, more and more intense until you reach your shoulder...

4. When you reach your shoulder, quickly move your fingers back to your wrist and repeat the process, increasing the intensity of your experience as you move slowly up your arm.

5. Repeat this two or three more times. Really enjoy your heightened state. You may be surprised at the intensity of good feelings that you can generate.

6. If you wish, set an anchor so that you can enjoy this wonderful feeling whenever and wherever you want.

Adding Spice
20 *There's a Heroine* in the **yellow zone** set the anchor.

Turn to this exercise to know and appreciate what really matters to you. Use it:

If you feel betrayed
If others aren't doing what you want
If you just can't understand where other people are coming from
If other people don't live up to your expectations
If other people just don't do what you want them to do

At the essential core of the feminine being is a tender, compassionate, nurturing heart, so ask yourself *"What really matters to me? What kind of woman do I ultimately want to become in my lifetime? What do my values need to be in order to achieve my ultimate destiny?"*

Values are the principles, the standards, ethics or ideals which we individually prize and consider vital to our well-being as we live our lives. No two person's values are identical, but they form the very basis of our health, our wealth, our relationships, our career and even the language we use. Yet, how often do we realise that many of the disagreements we have with others stem from a difference in core values? What is important to us may be of no importance to our life partner or a colleague at work. We assume or expect others to share our values, and this is simply not the case. It can lead to disappointment or betrayal. In fact, betrayal is what we do to ourselves when we expect someone else to live by our values and not their own.

The list of 49 values overleaf is not complete in itself; there may be other values you may feel are important to you. Go through the list and pick out your top 10, those which are most important to you and remember, the meaning you give these values is your own.

Time Taken: 10 minutes to set up; 5 second reminders during the day

1. Now take your top 10 and whittle them down to 7. When you are clear about your values, it's so much easier to make life choices; it will help you keep out of your life what you don't want, and invite

119

in what you do want. These 7 now become the values through which you can live your life.

2. Write out your values on sheets of paper in big letters, put them on the wall and look at them every day, or choose one per day or one per week and live your day/week with that value uppermost in your mind both at work and in your personal life, until each becomes so deeply ingrained in how you behave and who you become. When we do this, we take our life to a new level – we take it out of that awful state of mediocrity.

Your values are not set in stone – some may change as you progress through your journey of life, and that is just the way it is supposed to be.

Values

Achievement	Abundance
Acceptance	Advancement
Adventure	Aesthetics
Affection	Aliveness and Vitality
Authenticity	Balance
Beauty	Competitiveness
Contribution/Service	Cooperation
Creativity	Economic Security
Fame	Family Happiness
Freedom	Friendship
Fulfilment	Happiness

Health	Honesty
Humour	Independence
Inner Harmony	Integrity
Intimacy	Justice
Kindness	Leadership
Love	Mastery
Peace of Mind	Recognition
Respect	Romance
Safety and Security	Self-reliance
Simplicity	Sharing
Spirituality	Status
Success	Trust

| Uniqueness | | Wealth |
| Wisdom | | |

This exercise gives you some powerful tools for creating the life and lifestyle you want. Use it:

> *If you're fed up with getting more of the same in your life*
> *If you want to get what you want for a change*
> *When you want to create a vision and set goals for your future*
> *When you want your dreams to come true*

So often, our present circumstances reinforce the view we have of ourselves. Our job, our home or the car we drive come to define who we are and what we feel we are worth. If the best we can do is a beat-up old car that constantly breaks down, then we can come to see that as a measure of our worth.

And there's no need for that. You see, you can have anything that you truly want, anything that is right for you right now and that is in keeping rather than in conflict with what you most value. All you have to do is put your attention on it. In fact, the reason you continue to get more of the same in your life is because you continue to put your attention on your present circumstances, rather than on what you want. Your present circumstances are actually the hangover from your previous thoughts and behaviours.

That's where this exercise can help you. It works on the principle of let's pretend, a game we all played when we were kids. And it works in the same way as *"Open Your Eyes and See"*, in that it helps you attract into your life the good things and feelings you want to experience. You simply create and step into a dream – just for a minute or so. Each time you do it, you open yourself up to receiving what you dream of, and what you focus on begins to materialise in your life.

Almira plays this game when she's driving. For a minute or so, she imagines herself in the driving seat of a brand new Porsche 911 Carerra, with the roof down. She soaks up the sun, feels the warm breeze caress her face. She smells the new cream leather seats; gives a huge grin to her husband in the passenger seat. She turns the ignition, hears the engine purr then roar into life, and thrills with the excitement of racing it down country lanes. Then she drops the fantasy, before anything else intrudes into the virtual reality she has created for herself.

WARNING: This is an immensely powerful activity that always brings you exactly what you think about. Only use it with good feelings. *Never attempt to solve a problem with it.* There are plenty of other activities in the book for that purpose.

Before you begin, take time to read through the exercise and make a point to notice the sights, sounds, sensations, tastes and smells when you play this game.

Time Taken: 1 minute maximum

1. Imagine yourself in a scene of your own choosing, and day-dream in detail. This works best when that scene is allied to what you are experiencing now. If you're at work, it's a brief excursion into your dream job. Really get into the experience. Use the questions below to remind you what to pay attention to on your one minute voyage.

2. Look around. Create your surroundings in as much detail as possible.

    Where are you?
    What do you see?
    Who is with you?
    What are they wearing?
    How do they look at you?
    What do you hear?
    What do you feel?
    Is it hot, cold, dry, wet?

3. Pay attention to what you conjure up. The very fact that they are there means that they are meant to come into your awareness to tell you that you can have them.

4. As you get into this, you'll feel wonderful feelings that well up inside you.

5. If you bring someone into your dream, remember, it is because you choose to have them there to share this beautiful moment with you.

6. Spend a moment there, enjoying yourself to the full.

7. Come back **now** into present time awareness so you keep that great feeling inside you.

Adding Spice

36 *Open your Eyes and See* in the **indigo zone** to appreciate what you already have.

40   Let's Pretend!

This exercise helps you create the life of your dreams. Use it:

*If you're tired of getting more of the same in your life
and want a change
When you want to create your vision and set your goals
When you want to live the life of your dreams*

Do you recall playing let's pretend games as a child? We've all done it – got together with a few other children and created whatever experiences we wanted – doctors and nurses, cowboys and Indians in the Wild West, or made up a truly magical world for ourselves that no one could share unless we invited them in. At some stage in our lives, we stopped pretending and got real. And the magic was gone.

Yet, the magic of make-believe is very much at your disposal any time you choose to call upon it. And doing the adult form of *'Let's Pretend!'* is powerful stuff. You see, when you can play this game with the playfulness of a child and the commitment of an adult, you discover the magic of making dreams come true. You learn how to create whatever you want in your life, attracting to yourself only those things, only those people, and only those experiences that you most desire. You learn how to change your thinking and master your mind today to create the world of your dreams tomorrow.

Before you begin, buy a special notebook and reserve it for this exercise in creating the future you desire.

Time Taken: 10 – 15 minutes a day

1. Let's pretend you're a writer, a great writer with a gift for creating compelling tales of romance, mystery and adventure, of real people in real situations that interest and excite you.

2. Let's pretend that whatever you write is performed, and you get to choose how – the stage, film or television.

3. Let's pretend you're the heroine and the star. All the action revolves around you.

4. Begin to write your story, the story of the life you really want to live. You need to develop the background, characters and plot – and of course those recurring themes that are pivotal in your story.

5. Background first. Where do you live? Take time to describe your surroundings. Great writers fill in lots of sensory detail – colours, textures, scents, sounds, feelings. What kind of a house do you live in? Where is it located? Describe your neighbourhood.

6. The Heroine: Who are you? What are you really like? What does your body look and feel like? What have you accomplished? What do you value? How do you grow and develop?

7. Characters: Who is with you? Who are your nearest and dearest? Who are your neighbours, your friends and acquaintances, your colleagues at work? Take time to describe the people you have in your life – and the ones you want to attract into it. What do they look like? What qualities do they possess? How will you know when you've met them? What will you see, hear or feel when they walk into the room? How do they treat you? Great writers are good at building character. Allow yours to grow and develop too.

8. What do you do together? Go through a typical day. What do you eat? What do you do with your time? Where do you work? What experiences and adventures do you have? What's it like to be you, living the life of your dreams?

9. Once you have the basic outline of the life you want to live – and it may take a week or two to write all this down – begin to live it each day. When you step into your car, imagine it's the one you plan to have. When you collect the kids from school, hug them and greet them the way you would in your story. When you're

at work, begin doing the things that really make your heart sing, and notice the daily improvements in your life.

10. Keep adding to your story. The richer you make it, the more detail you include, the more real it will become to you, and the sooner you'll begin to manifest it in your life.

Adding Spice

To supplement your story, and make it more real, check out some of these exercises: *39 Virtual Reality* and *41 Postage Stamp* both in the **indigo zone.**

This exercise puts your goal into automatic pilot so that you cannot help but achieve it. Success is guaranteed. Use it:

If you have a habit of setting goals and not achieving them
Whenever you set a goal

Often, we set goals for ourselves and never seem to accomplish them. We begin with enthusiasm, and as time goes on, we lose our excitement and commitment. We may even choose to drop the goal, comforting ourselves by saying we really didn't want it anyway.

This need never be the case again. The secret is to decide what you want, make it so desirable it captivates your imagination, and then install it into your mind to run on automatic pilot for you. When you stay focused, you achieve what you desire.

Now that you've become aware of your thinking, and adept at noticing and appreciating all the good that surrounds you, you probably have a much better idea of what kind of life and lifestyle you want for yourself. How you want to feel, the experiences you love, the people you have, and those you want to attract into your life, the work you are drawn to do, the contribution you want to make. Be clear about what you want.

When you can complete this exercise, you discover you've made a switch between where you are now and where you want to be. You've programmed your unconscious mind to accept your goal or future lifestyle as the way things are. And now, because of the way your mind works, it will take your desired goal as fact, and deliver on it for you.

Before you begin, and as a pre-requisite to this exercise, write your goal or future lifestyle down in as much sensory detail as possible. Use *Virtual Reality* and *Let's Pretend* on each aspect of it, to get really clear about what you want before you begin.

Time Taken: 5 to 10 minutes

1. Find a place where you won't be disturbed

2. Close your eyes and bring into your mind's eye an image of the way you live now. Let it fill an imaginary television screen in front of you. Make this screen as big as you can.

3. Notice that in the top left hand corner of the screen, there is a small image of your goal or future lifestyle, about the size of a postage stamp

4. Now take hold of the postage stamp image and pull it towards you, as if it were on a huge elastic band. Keep stretching it, and stretching it

5. Let it go! The images swap over on the screen. Now your future state is on the big screen and your present state a tiny postage stamp in the corner.

6. Step into your goal or future lifestyle. See it, hear it, feel all those wonderful feelings. Get involved. Move around. Act as if you have your goal or your future lifestyle right now.

7. When you're done, step out and repeat the exercise, maybe even as many as 20 times, beginning at step 2, until you can no longer bring up your original lifestyle. The way you are now is gone.

8. This means your brain is re-programmed. It believes you already have your goal or future lifestyle and acts on it. All you have to do is continue to take the next step in achieving it.

Adding Spice

Get clear on your goals with *39 Virtual Reality* and *40 Let's Pretend* both in the **indigo zone.**

Chapter 7

The New You

Chapter 7   The New You

Are you successful, yet feel there's something missing?
Do you ever ask yourself, "Is this it?"
Or, "Is this all there is to life?"
Do you ever wonder why you're here?

If so, you're in the **violet zone**, searching for a greater purpose in your life, wanting to make a greater contribution, searching for meaning, if only you could find it.

That something missing is your sense of purpose – an answer to the question *"Why am I here?"* The answer to this question is really important to our self-esteem, for *when we live and work on purpose, we constantly feed our self-worth.* We realise that the contribution we make to others is meaningful and valued, and that we are valued – by ourselves and by others. Living and working from this level ensures success in any venture we undertake.

For a lucky few, finding their purpose is easy. We're sure you've come across them – they effortlessly fall into a role, a profession or a business that is absolutely right for them, and sail through life full of joy, excitement and enthusiasm.

For most of us, it takes much longer, often because we seldom give ourselves the time – or the right process – to discover the work we were born to do. In this final chapter, we invite you to take that time, and use these powerful exercises to uncover the meaning and explore the purpose in your life. That's what the **violet zone** is about.

Violet is the colour of vision and inner guidance, of being all we can be, the colour of life's meaning and purpose. In the **violet zone**, you will find exercises and tools that encourage you to be at your best, to discover and live your true purpose so that you can be all you are meant to be, to trust your intuition and the guidance it gives you. Living on purpose, in grateful awareness of all that you have and are, you truly can and do esteem yourself.

When you can complete all the exercises in this chapter, you put meaning back in your life and begin to live on purpose. There is no greater gift you can give yourself than permission to do what you – with your unique skills, talents and experience – came into this precious world to accomplish. As you live on purpose, you uncover your passion and approach everything in your life with renewed energy and vigour.

1. You begin to attract people and resources to you. They see your passion, resonate with your purpose and want to join you on your mission. Be grateful for their contribution.

2. You learn to acknowledge and trust a higher order to support you as you do your life's work. And from that space, you discover the magic of being in the flow. You realise that when you live and work with purpose, you strengthen your self-esteem and ensure your success.

This activity, performed daily, will shift your awareness and bring more joy, peace and happiness into your life. Use it:

If you get to the end of the day wondering is this all there is?
When you're looking for meaning in your life
When you want to experience more joy and happiness
If you're bored with your lot
If you feel your life is dull and monotonous

Although there are times when our lives may seem dull, there is always something we can find to be thankful for, even if it's just the faint smell of a rose wafting across the night air. When we take the time to acknowledge that one small thing, we make a shift in our awareness – a significant change in our attitude that opens us up to noticing and appreciating all the good things in our life.

An attitude of Gratitude is probably the most important means we have to real wealth and abundance – an inner wealth, joy, health and well-being. When we are grateful for what we have in our lives we attract and experience even more happiness. That in turn, gives us more to be grateful for, and before we know it, we're attracting more and more of those wonderful feelings, people and fulfilment into our lives.

And when we're happy, we tend to be doing what we love – which is the best indicator we have for knowing and living on purpose. So, when you can take time every day to do this exercise, you learn to feel grateful for what you have, and get better at finding things to be grateful for. As if by magic – and it is magical and at the same time very real – you begin to attract more of what brings you joy, peace and happiness. And in those moments of gratitude, you begin to feel drawn – through those good feelings – to the path you are meant to follow.

Never underestimate the power of this exercise. Gratitude heals. Gratitude nourishes. Gratitude and love are the greatest healers on the planet.

Before you begin, buy yourself a special notebook or diary as your Gratitude Journal.

Time Taken: Approximately 10 to15 minutes a day

1. At the end of the day, take out your Gratitude Journal and write in it at least 10 things that you are grateful for today.

2. As you write them in your journal, take a moment to savour that experience again and say thank you for it. They might be tiny things or big things. Think and be grateful about these blessings until you have tears of gratitude in your eyes.

3. Keep this awareness with you through the next day. You are blessed and the more you realise this and experience it deep inside you, the more likely you are to be further blessed with good things.

Play this game to set a goal that really means something to you, one which makes your heart sing. Turn to it:

> *If you're in the habit of setting goals and never achieving them*
> *If you feel you're wandering aimlessly without*
> *a goal or vision to focus on*
> *If you tend to put off doing the very things*
> *you need to realise your goals*
> *If you've ever achieved a goal and wondered why you*
> *ever bothered – it's not what you want*
> *If you tend to give up on a goal once the going gets tough*

To achieve a goal that really means something to us, we need to have the right one – one that we know will bring us the satisfaction and fulfilment we desire. We also need to keep focused on that goal, so that we continue to move towards it, regardless of the resistance we experience from ourselves and those around us.

This exercise works by getting you to step into your future and rehearse what it's like to achieve your goals and dreams. It also tells you very quickly – in a matter of a few minutes – whether what you desire really is right for you. You know this immediately. All you need do is trust your feelings and intuition. When you feel good, you are aligned with your desires. When you feel uncomfortable, awkward or unfulfilled in any way, take this as a clear sign that your goal is not right for you.

Indeed, when you can play your *Dress Rehearsal* often, you'll see a huge shift in your awareness. You become more confident in your direction, positive and focused in your work and more relaxed in all that you do. And as you keep rehearsing, your dreams soon begin to materialise in your life. You cannot get too much of this.

Before you begin, take some time to decide what you want to achieve.

Time Taken: Less than five minutes, as frequently as you like

1. Go to a place where you feel comfortable and won't be disturbed. You will need a few feet of free space in front of you.

2. Stand comfortably, relax and as far as possible, let go of your thoughts.

3. Gently bring your attention to one of your dreams or goals.

4. Imagine a circle on the floor a few feet in front of you that represents your dream or goal. In a few moments you are going to step into that circle, and when you do, you have achieved your goal. It's yours to enjoy.

5. For now stay where you are and imagine yourself stepping into that goal.

6. Observe yourself closely. What do you look like once you've achieved your goals? What are you doing? What are you saying? Where are you? Who is with you? How do you feel? Feel how you would feel if you've really got there, if this dream or goal was truly fulfilled.

7. If it feels wrong, STOP. It's not for you!

8. If it feels right, take the next step. Physically step into your dream. Take a step forward into the circle, and merge with your dream, with the you who has achieved your goal or reached the next big step on the path to that goal.

9. Breathe that feeling of success into your body. What's it like to be here having achieved your dream? In your imagination take a look around you. Pay attention to all you see and hear. Feel the sensations, the emotions of having achieved your goal. Drink it all in.

10. If it feels wrong, STOP and step out.

11. If it feels right, bring in the rest of your cast – any people, and objects, any experiences that are a part of your dream. Savour, enjoy and appreciate this experience. Create this exactly the way you want.

12. When you are ready, come out

This simple exercise helps you clear your to-do list effortlessly, by trusting that you are not alone and are supported in all you do. Use it:

If you're juggling too much
If your to-do list keeps growing and you never get it cleared!
If you find it hard to delegate
If you feel you're the only one who can do what you have to do

As working women, we juggle work and home, sometimes wondering if our hectic lives will ever let up. There always seems to be more to do in a day than there are hours available. Even though the to-do list is impossible to squeeze into a day, we somehow feel it's our fault that we don't get everything done. And there's nothing more damaging for our self-esteem than to feel inadequate!

There's a simple answer. Do what is really important, delegate what others are good at and leave the rest. Anything amongst the rest that needs to be done will get done – just not by you. The rest doesn't matter. When you can complete this exercise regularly, you discover what is important for you to do, and what can be left for others – or just forgotten. The pressure is off and you begin to work more in your flow, playing to your strengths, doing what you are good at and leaving others to do what they are good at. As you become practiced in this, you find that others pick up the rest of the items on your to-do list without being asked.

In playing this game, we're asking you to take a risk and see what happens. It will develop your ability to trust your intuition, and discover that some higher power really will deliver to you what you want and need.

Before you begin, make a copy of the diary page overleaf. You may find *Let's Pretend!* or *Dress Rehearsal* helps you get clear about what's really important for you.

Time Taken: A few minutes every morning, or last thing at night

1. Make a list of all the things you have to do today, or if doing this last thing at night, things you have to do tomorrow.

2. Go through your list and mark those which are distractions and put them in the *Distractions* column. And forget about them.

3. Then review the list again, picking out all those tasks you know that you can delegate, and write those in the *Delegate* column.

4. In the *Only I Can Do* column write down the things which you are truly the only person who can do because of your skills and talents and passion, together with the things that make your heart sing.

5. Turn everything else on the list over to the Universe. Yes, the Universe – some higher power that can and does support you. Crazy though this may sound to you, we ask only that you take a risk for a day or two and trust in the process. The Universe actually will look after it, or you'll find you just don't need it. When you let go of these things, the pressure and strain of having to do them will fall away.

6. Do what's on your *Only I Can Do* list – the ones only you can do, the ones you know you can complete today, and allow yourself to feel good about accomplishing them.

7. Watch in amazement as the activities in the *For the Universe* column get done without your help or interference. You may find that a colleague at work offers to take one of those pressing – and boring – jobs off your hands or that the situation changes and you no longer need to prepare that lengthy report after all.

Adding Spice

40 *Let's Pretend* in the **indigo zone** and 43 *Dress Rehearsal* in the **violet zone.**

Diary for To Do or Not to Do

Date:_____

Only I Can Do	Delegate	Distractions	For the Universe

This exercise draws out your highest energies and makes them available to you as you live on purpose. Use it:

Whenever you want or need a quick pick-me-up of energy
If you lose focus and need to regain it
If you're off-balance and need to restore your energy levels
When you need to solve problems that require your creativity and/or insights

Drawing sideways figures of eight helps the energy in your body cross over from left to right and right to left which balances and harmonises you and restores your focus and concentration. It also opens you up to creativity and insights.

Time Taken: 1 - 2 minutes

1. Stand up and trace a sideways figure of eight in the air with your right hand, running your arm upwards through the mid-point of the eight. This direction lifts your energy. Sweep your arm out wide to the right and wide to the left. Follow it with your eyes and the whole of your body. See the diagram on the next page.

2. Repeat at least a dozen times.

3. Use your left hand to trace the same sideways figure of eight in the air, again sweeping your arm up through the centre of the eight, and as far to the left and right as possible.

4. Finish by using both hands to sweep the figure of eight. Repeat at least 12 times.

5. You can also walk the pattern of a figure of eight along the carpet several times which will restore harmony and peace to your body and mind and open you up to greater awareness and creativity.

6. If you are at work and unable to do this physically, use a pencil and paper and trace out the figure of eight on it, first with your right hand, then your left, and then both, following the movement with your eyes. This is not quite as effective, but it still works.

Adding Spice

In tracing the figure of eight, run from bottom left to top right (through the dark bit) then around from bottom right to top left.

This amazing activity gives you precious insights into the meaning and purpose of your life. Use it:

> *When you want to find meaning and purpose in your life*
> *If you're successful, but something's missing*
> *Whenever you're looking for direction*
> *When you want to understand just how and why you tick*

Just because you're really good at your job doesn't mean that it's what you're here for. We've all been tempted to carry on doing a job we're brilliant at because of the status it gives us and the pay packet which supports the role. Yet in our heart we know there must be something more to life than this.

What would it be like for you to do the work you were born to do – work that makes you jump for joy, work that allows you to make the contribution that only you can make, because you are in your flow? When you're in your flow, you are doing what you are best at doing; you are doing what you love. And that gives your work purpose and meaning. It can't help but make your heart sing.

The first step is to recall times when you were at your best, feeling amazing and fulfilled and loving what you were doing. In the second stage, you walk through a series of logical levels, so that you can gain clarity and insights into what really matters to you. You'll discover where and when you are at your best, what you do, the skills and talents you bring into play and the beliefs and values you hold.

Importantly, you discover *who you really are* when you are at your best, and go beyond that to gain insights into the meaning and purpose you bring to the world in the contribution you make.

Having gained that clarity and understanding, and with all those insights, you then retrace your steps, integrating that understanding into every aspect of your life.

Time taken: 15 to 20 minutes, first time through; 10 minutes thereafter

Stage 1

1. Find a place where you will not be disturbed. You will need enough floor space to take six paces back and forth across the room.

2. Take six pieces of paper, and label them

   Sheet 1: ENVIRONMENT
   Sheet 2: BEHAVIOUR
   Sheet 3: SKILLS & CAPABILITIES
   Sheet 4: VALUES & BELIEFS
   Sheet 5: IDENTITY
   Sheet 6: BEYOND IDENTITY

3. Lay them out from 1 to 6 in a straight line in front of you.

4. Read through the instructions before you begin. You may wish to write your answers down. If so, make sure you have pen and paper to hand. Otherwise, trust your unconscious mind to deliver the answers and insights to you as you need them.

Stage 2

1. Recall at least three times when you were at your best. These do not have to be grand things. They are just times when you knew, unequivocally, that you were in your flow. You were doing what you loved, and it was easy and effortless.

2. When you are ready, and with your "being at your best" experiences in mind, take the first step into your environment and ask yourself:

Environment	"Where are you when you are being your best?"
	"When are you when you are being at your best?"
	"Who are you with when you are being at your best?"

3. Take all the time you need to experience the where, when and with whom of being at your best. Get as much detail as you can.

4. When you're ready, take the next step into behaviour. Again, thinking of being at your best, ask yourself:

Behaviour	*"What do you do when you are being at your best?"*

5. Take time to experience what you are *actually doing* when you're at your best.

6. When you're ready, step forward into your skills and capabilities, your talents and ask yourself:

Capability	*"What skills and capabilities do you draw on when you are being at your best?"*
	"What talents are you using?"

7. Take as long as you need to answer these questions. When you are ready, take another step forward into your values and beliefs and ask:

Beliefs	*"What do you believe and what values do you hold dear when you are being at your best?"*

8. Answer these questions fully. When you are ready, take the next step into your identity. This is who you are. Take your time to ask yourself:

Identity	*"Who are you when you are being at your best?"*

10. Now go beyond identity. This is where you step beyond yourself, beyond the trappings of your personality into an experience that

is more spiritual in its nature – a place that holds meaning for you.

| Beyond Identity | "Who are you when you are being at your best beyond identity?" |

"What is your mission when you are being at your best beyond identity?"

"What is the vision you are pursuing or representing when you are being at your best beyond identity?"

"Who else or what else are you serving when you are being at your best beyond identity?"

11. Take your time to answer these questions. When you are ready, gather up all the awareness you have received, and begin to retrace your steps. Taking everything you have learned and experienced with you, step back into identity...

| Identity | "Who are you when you are being at your best?" |

12. Pay attention to your answers. They are likely to be so much more profound and meaningful to you and make a note of them.

13. When you're ready, and taking with you everything you have learned and experienced from beyond identity and from identity, step back into your values and beliefs and ask yourself:

| Beliefs | "What do you believe and what values do you hold dear when you are being at your best?" |

14. Pay attention to your insights and answers. When you are ready, and taking everything you have learned with you, step back into your capabilities.

Capability	"What skills and capabilities do you draw on when you are being at your best?"
	"What talents are you using?"

15. Slowly move on. Taking everything that you have learned with you, step back into your behaviour.

Behaviour	"What do you do when you are being at your best?"

16. Again, pay attention to your insights. And taking everything that you have learned with you, step back into your environment and ask:

Environment	"Where are you when you are being your best?"
	"When are you when you are being at your best?"
	"Who are you with when you are being at your best?"

17. You will be amazed by the insights you have received, and know what really matters to you and how best it is for you to pursue that to put meaning and purpose into your work and your life.

Now that you've come to the end of this particular journey, it's time to acknowledge what you have accomplished and treat yourself.

You've overcome your fears of rejection, of looking a fool
You have cleared old patterns of behaviour that kept you stuck
You've learned to handle criticism and set and maintain your boundaries
You've improved your body image and built your self-esteem and self-worth
You've learned to nurture yourself and to support others in growing their self-esteem
You've come to understand the power of your words, and how you can use them to get what you want
You've learned to create your vision and set goals you can easily achieve
You've found meaning and purpose to feed and nourish your growing self-worth

Now it's time to celebrate – by doing something different – something you haven't done before or at least not for a long while, something that makes your heart sing. Here are a few suggestions, or find your own very special way to acknowledge yourself for completing this challenging yet rewarding journey with us. Trust yourself and your new found self-esteem, and do whatever pleases you.

1. If you've never travelled alone before, take a short day trip on your own and enjoy it…or jump on Eurostar, or catch a plane to a European city and explore.

2. Treat yourself to a colour and style consultation – a new image to match your new-found sense of self.

3. Buy yourself an outfit that really suits you. What you have in your wardrobe may still project the old self-image, not the new you. Enjoy wearing your new clothes.

4. Or wear a colour that you haven't worn before. And pay attention to how you feel and how others respond to you...

5. Buy yourself some delicious new underwear that suits your new sensual self.

6. Take up a painting class...

7. Or learn to belly dance...

8. Or gardening, or wine tasting, or...

9. Go for a hot air balloon ride.

10. Have a horse-riding lesson.

11. Treat yourself to a day at the spa.

12. Have your make-up done.

13. Go hang-gliding.

14. Join a club or network and socialise.

15. Really accept a compliment – something we women find hard to do. Acknowledge it, thank the person, let it sink in, feel good about it.

16. Wear something outrageous – just once for a dare and see how you feel.

17. When you hear yourself saying "*I could never do that!*" Instead say "*I could never do that yet*" and gently ask yourself when you could. When the time is right, do it.

18. If you tend to hang back at a party or social gathering, walk up to someone and strike up a conversation.

19. Volunteer to give a presentation.

20. Take an afternoon off and do nothing.

21. Have a day in bed with a glass of champagne and some strawberries and a juicy novel.

Or whatever you want. Go on – you deserve it – you really do.

Thank you for joining us on this adventure into the unknown. We trust you have enjoyed the stay and will continue to learn and grow.

When you want to discover even more amazing, untapped resources in your life, come to one of our Rainbow days, or register for one-to-one coaching with Almira or Susie. Please visit our website, www.path-to-freedom.com/resources for more details.

We look forward to sharing time with you again.

Susie Heath

Susie Heath is a relationship coach, a clinical hypnotherapist, certified NLP practitioner and dance therapist. She has used this extraordinary set of skills in coaching hundreds of women over the past 10 years, working with them to improve their self-confidence and self-esteem. Now a highly trained, skilled and experienced corporate and life coach, and author of "**The Essence of Womanhood**", she specialises in vision and purpose, and relationship and intimacy coaching.

Her working career has been varied – with high powered roles in the corporate world, and running her own successful businesses. She has taught French, been a fashion buyer for a large high street store and a production assistant with a film company. While bringing up her three children, she ran her own horticultural company for 14 years from home. After her divorce, she trained in clinical hypnotherapy and coaching and has been working extensively with women ever since.

She and Almira met on the Educo™ Mind Masters seminar in June of 2006, after which they decided to combine their experience and expertise to create **Written in the Rainbow: A Woman's Secret to Self-Esteem.**

Almira Ross

Almira Ross is an author, inspirational speaker and well-respected business coach. She is a certified practitioner of NLP (NeuroLinguistic Programming), a graduate of Landmark and Insight, an Educo™ Mind Master and a liveryman of the City of London.

Almira spent 25 years in the IT industry, working her way to the top only to discover she'd lost her soul somewhere along the way... Five years ago, she plucked up the courage to leave the corporate world and make a career of her life-long passion for self-development. She has been coaching individuals and business men and women ever since, encouraging them to discover their purpose, and set their lives – and businesses – on fire.

In particular, she has worked with hundreds of women to help them recover their self-confidence and self-esteem. Combining this extensive experience and expertise with that of Susie Heath, she has co-authored the first of several books to support women in the work environment. **Written in the Rainbow: a Woman's Secret to Self-Esteem** is the first of seven books to be published in the series.

She and Susie also run energy workshops and Rainbow Days for women.

Written in the Rainbow

Written in the Rainbow: A Woman's Secret to Self-Esteem is the first in a series of seven books devoted to women who work. Colour coded from red, through all the colours of the rainbow, each of these books deals with specific issues that we women so often face in our lives – and provides easy, practical ways to overcome them. Written by women, specifically for women, they touch at the very heart of who we are and what matters most to us in our hectic, overstretched lives.

Written in the Rainbow Titles

A Woman's Secret to Handling Stress – in which you learn to overcome your early – and inappropriate – conditioning and discover how to manage the expectations other people place on you easily and effortlessly. You'll find in it a wealth of tools and techniques for avoiding stress, for managing your personal state, your time, your energy and the people around you. You'll discover how to relax body and mind and regain your personal power.

A Woman's Secret to Unleashing Your Creativity – which encourages you to recognize and appreciate your immense creativity, draw it out from within and begin to use it effectively in your every day life. You'll learn brainstorming and decision making techniques, build your confidence and come to recognize and appreciate the creative energy in male/female relationships.

A Woman's Secret to Self-Esteem – a set of exercises and activities to develop your confidence and build healthy self-esteem, with tools and techniques to heal past trauma and fix knee-jerk reactions. You'll discover and come to nurture and love the great woman that you are. You'll know your boundaries; you'll learn to respect yourself. And once you do, others will automatically respect your boundaries and cherish you for who you are.

A Woman's Secret to Balancing Home and Work – which encourages you to address and resolve conflicts that arise from all the demands placed on you at home and at work. You'll learn to recognize, and where appropriate, re-define, other people's expectations of you – and yours of them. You'll learn to set boundaries, nurture yourself, care for those who most matter to you, and develop meaningful, nurturing relationships with your partner, your children (if you have them), your colleagues and friends.

A Woman's Secret to Success in the Workplace – begins with tools and techniques to help you remove the limitations to your success and unleash your creative potential. In it, you'll learn effective ways to communicate with others – how to use your voice and body for expressive and desired impact. You'll discover "The Physiology of Success"™ and learn to integrate this into every cell of your body so that you live and breathe it every day. You'll discover the secrets to team dynamics, and how you – with your unique skills and experience – can best make your contribution to your team. You'll develop your vision and leadership skills.

A Woman's Secret to Realising Your Full Potential – packed with tools and techniques to help you clear away any left-over issues and repetitive patterns that are holding you back, before embarking on an amazing voyage of personal discovery and growth. You'll create your vision and discover your purpose; you'll come to understand your values and how to work with them to achieve that vision. You'll discover how to identify and attract to you the people you need in your life and begin to live a life on purpose. In short, you'll put meaning and fulfilment back into your life.

A Woman's Secret to Energy and Vitality – in which you will discover one of the greatest secrets of all time – how to replenish your energy, boost your vitality and come alive in a way that is irresistible to all those around you. You'll discover that what the world really needs is people who have come alive, and can spark that life within others – people with the *secret to energy and vitality* – people like you!

Please visit our website, www.path-to-freedom.com/resources for more information, or to let us know which of these titles most resonates with you. That way, we can incorporate your feedback into our writing and writing schedules.

Rainbow Days

Rainbow Days are run four times a year – in early February, May, August and November. When you attend a Rainbow Day, you'll step into a world where you have much needed and precious time for you – and you alone. Time for you to

- *Re-lax and re-treat from the world for a few hours to*
- *Re-plenish and re-store your energy and*
- *Re-balance your life*

You'll discover how to easily and effortlessly

- *Re-fresh, re-juvenate and re-new yourself*
- *Re-cognize and re-member how very special you are*
- *Re-joice as you re-gain your sacred sense of self and*
- *Re-cover and re-connect with your vision and purpose*

These are very special days created specially for women who work, and tailored to meet our women's needs at different times of the calendar year. Remember, as women we are sensitive, and acutely attuned to, the cycles of nature – the daily rhythms of light and darkness, the lunar rhythms that match our menstrual cycles, the yearly rhythms of the seasons. And it's important that we acknowledge our natural cycles and re-attune ourselves with those of the world around us to re-store balance to our hectic lives.

For more information and to register for one of our Rainbow Days, please visit our website, www.path-to-freedom.com/resources.

The Essence of Womanhood – re-awakening the authentic feminine

Women – have you forgotten who you are? Ever wish you had an instruction manual for yourself? Feel there is part of you missing? Spent years battling your way up the ladder in the corporate market or being chauffeur, decorator and skivvy bringing up your children?

Susie Heath's book *The Essence of Womanhood – re-awakening the authentic feminine* is the book you've been waiting for.

+ Reveal the gorgeous, beautiful, powerful, feminine being you were born to be, and let her out to play!

+ Clear away your unconscious limiting beliefs that have prevented you living the life of your dreams

+ Become an attraction magnet for men in your life

+ Use your mind and body in new and exciting ways

+ Fall in love with both the inner and outer you

+ Enjoy every moment of being a real woman, however many times you have been around the sun

………and many more essential answers about love, life, your body and feeling like a natural woman.

"The author has managed to beautifully combine profound concepts with practical exercises that ensure the leap from intellectual appreciation to a real understanding of what it means to be feminine. Her light and humorous style makes it very easy to read. This is a fabulous book and one I would thoroughly recommend to any woman who wants to really know herself."

Kate Mottershead, Hampshire

Order your copy of *The Essence of Womanhood* NOW
www.essenceofwomanhood.com
or from www.amazon.co.uk www.ecademy-press.co.uk
Waterstones, or any good book store

Printed in Great Britain
by Amazon